LEATHERWORK

LEATHERWORK
IAN HAMILTON-HEAD

Photography by Paul Broadhurst
Line drawings by Carole Vincent

Blandford Press · Poole Dorset

First published 1979
© 1979 Blandford Press Ltd
Link House, West Street
Poole, Dorset, BH15 1LL

ISBN 0 7137 0928 6

British Library Cataloguing in Publication Data
Hamilton-Head, Ian
    Leatherwork.
    1. Leather work
    I. Title
    745.53'1   TT290

Set in 11/12 Plantin, printed and bound in Great Britain by
Cox and Wyman Ltd,
London, Fakenham and Reading

Contents

This book is dedicated to all the leathercraftsmen of the past, present and future whose love of the material has enhanced our craft.

Acknowledgements

I should like to thank all the people who made this book possible; Blandford Press for approaching me to write it and turning an idea into a reality, and Paul Broadhurst and Carole Vincent whose photographs and line drawings do great credit to showing leather-work at its best. I thank them for their diligent work and their help and suggestions. My biggest thanks must go to Shirley Bridgwater who, in between bringing up a young family, has had to contend with correcting my spelling mistakes, as well as ploughing through my often ungrammatical and unintelligible writing, to type the manuscript and make it make sense. Finally I must thank my wife, Tricia, for all the help and encouragement she has given as well as putting up with me when things were not going right.

Ian Hamilton-Head

Introduction

Leather is one of the oldest materials known to man, and without it he may not have survived. Prehistoric man used to kill for meat, and found he could clothe himself, make bedding, boats (coracles) and shelter himself from the rain with animal skins. His main problem was to preserve them and stop them from rotting, so he started to look for ways in which to do this by trying salting and smoking them (in a similar way to how fish and meats are smoked), but they remained hard and brittle, and lasted only a short time before putrefying. We do not know the exact way man discovered the art of preserving hide, turning it into a primitive type of leather. It could have been that while experimenting with different herbs and berries to eat and drink he stumbled on to stewing-up the bark of the oak tree into a liquor, similar to the way you would make tea today; then, finding the taste nasty, perhaps he threw the liquor away to where a pile of old skins lay discarded from the animals he had slaughtered for food. When he found that the skins on to which he had thrown the liquor had preserved better than others, he was at the beginning of a very primitive form of oak bark tanning. Hard to believe maybe, but no wilder a theory than the way many things are believed to have evolved. Man then went on to use other methods of curing and tanning, such as rubbing Alum (mineral salt) into the hide from which he had first removed the hair with a sharp stone (similar to shaving), or Lime, which would burn the hair off. He would then end up with a white leather; this process is called tawing.

Through thousands of years man went on to find many many more ways of curing and tanning animal, reptile, and even fish skins, as well as putting them to a wide variety of uses. Although the potter's craft is very old, long before this man was using leather mugs (blackjacks) to drink from, leather pouches to keep his food in, and even bottles, of a type, to store liquids in. Leathercraft predates nearly all other crafts, and articles which are fine examples of leathercraftmanship have been found that date back as far as ancient Egyptian times. Every civilisation in the world has used and uses leather, from Stone Age man who bound his feet with primitive hides out of necessity, to the luxurious leather upholstery of a Rolls-Royce car's seating. Leather has and will always be there.

The traditions of leathercraft and the people who have perpetuated them are wide and varied, but what they all have in common is their love and feel for the material. In recent years only we have had the varying styles of Old English saddlery, with its fine stitching and often very simple beauty, many examples of which may be seen at the Leather Museum in Walsall, England.

We have had the Western look of American leatherwork, with its ornate carvings and braiding (plaiting of leather thongs) work on gun holsters, saddle-bags and a great variety of other items, and we have also had the leatherwork from Turkey, India and Spain for a tourist market, often with geometric designs upon the items.

Then the great youth explosion came, when all young people wanted to do craftwork. The result was the multi-coloured leatherwork of the new youth culture, with its multi-embossing and fringing designs, etc.; often this work lacked the technical expertise of the older craftsmen, but it had an inspired vitality that so much of the more commercial leatherwork did not have.

In this book I intend to try to bring together many of the best qualities of all these techniques, and try to give a much more varied approach to leatherwork. In the following chapters you will learn about tools, materials and many processes, but always remember that it is your hands and ideas that are most important. You are not trying to cover the material and decorate it beyond recognition, but rather to enhance its natural beauty. I have been working with leather for ten years now, and have never ceased learning from new ideas and seeing new work. Through leatherwork I have met many interesting people in the pursuit of the craft of leather, also some very eccentric ones – such as one of England's top craftsmen, who learned his skills while serving a term in prison for bank robbery and who, I have often heard boast, was taught to carve leather by one of the best safe crackers in North America. I have also made many friends who have shared the secrets of the craft with me, and the love of the material leather.

I hope that through this book you may embark on an exciting adventure into leatherwork.

1   Making a Start

Work Space   The first thing you will need is a place to work; somewhere with light (preferably daylight) that is dry and clean, and with enough space to work easily. For a couple of years I used the kitchen floor for cutting-out, and the kitchen table for doing the assembly etc. and, although it is possible, I would not recommend it. It is better to get yourself somewhere to keep your leather and tools – a 'leather place', so to speak. Keep your leather away from direct heat and sunlight, and free from damp, as these are all harmful.

You will need a solid bench for cutting-out and generally working on, but it is best to have a cutting board which can be moved. A piece of zinc sheet about 30cm (2ft) square is perfect, as this will not blunt your knife, nor will it cut sufficiently to cause large grooves which your knife would run into. You will also need some way of storing your tools, rivets, etc. A tool rack can be either bought or made, and six or so tobacco tins will make ideal storage for things like rivets, needles, and so on. Alternatively you can use some screw-top coffee jars – by nailing the tops from the inside to the underside of a shelf you can then screw the jar up into it, making ideal storage containers for small items.

It is best to have a separate place for dyeing, as dye if spilt can make quite a mess of an unfinished bag or belt, not to mention your tools and materials.

In my experience though, it is the standard of your work by which you are judged and not the conditions in which you work; in fact, very often the best work is done in the worst conditions, but this is not a recommendation.

There are many leatherworking tools available. Some are merely **Basic Tools**
timesavers, and not entirely necessary, though often nice to have if
you can afford them. I can remember buying my first tools, going
into a shop in London which supplied them, and just pointing at
different tools and saying to the shop assistant 'I'll have that one,
now what does it do?' – not really the best way of going about it, so
I will list some of the tools needed by the beginner. For a wider
variety of tools available you will find at the back of the book an
extensive list of tool suppliers and manufacturers, many of whom
will be only too pleased to send you their catalogues. Be warned
though – their job is to sell tools, and the more they sell the happier
they are, so stop and think – often you can do the work of one tool
with another which you already have. Well – here goes – basic
tools:

A good steel ruler is preferable, at least 1 metre (about 3ft) long. *1 Ruler*
This you will need for cutting against, and measuring for making
patterns.

Fig. 1 Tools: a *ruler;* b *knife;* c *revolving punch plier;* d *scissors;* e *strap cutter;* f *hammer;*
g *screw crease;* h *edge shave;* j *awl;* k *stitch marker.*

2 Knife A clicker knife with detachable blade is best for all-round use as it has a small curved blade which is very good for more intricate work as well as larger cuts. Also, if you break a blade (which you are bound to do) you can replace it very cheaply. One can also use a 'Stanley' knife with a curved blade; it is not quite as versatile, but will do the job. Then there are the Saddler's round knife and half-round knife, both of which your tool supplier will demonstrate to you. As I have found that these take a lot of practice to be able to use properly, I would not recommend them for the beginner.

3 Revolving Punch Plier There are many punch pliers on the market, the best being the more solid types, although one can buy a cheap pressed steel version that will do the same job. I have used one of these for years, despite having a better one, as I find that being lighter it is easier to handle. The punches vary from 0–6 in size, and so make varying holes for stitching, lacing, and attaching various press-studs, rivets and catches. Always make sure before buying that the punches are sharp, and the revolving chamber does not slip round too easily, as this can be most infuriating as well as damaging your projects.

4 Scissors These must be good quality, as light substitutes will just not do the job of cutting heavier leather efficiently. I would recommend a pair of proper leather shears from one of the specialist leather tool firms. It is also handy to have a pair of ordinary household scissors for cutting paper and card pattern templates; on no account use your leather scissors for this, as it will blunt them.

5 Strap Cutter Strap cutters go under the name of plough knives, which are the better quality steel tools used for cutting belts and straps. A plough knife has an adjustable guide for cutting in various widths, and if you intend making quantities of belts or straps you will find it invaluable. It is fairly expensive, but there is, however, a cheaper wooden one called a 'stript-ease' which uses razor blades, is also adjustable, and will do the job fairly well, but is not so durable (see Tandy Leather Co. in the List of Suppliers p. 127). Of course you can always use a knife and ruler, but you must have a steady hand when cutting, otherwise your belt will end up with a very jerky edge. I used to cut belts by knife and ruler, but found that by investing in a plough knife it paid for itself fairly quickly by being faster and more efficient.

Its uses are numerous – banging in rivets, flattening stitches, attaching press-studs, and so on. Here I prefer a steel-shafted hammer, as they are almost indestructible, and if you have ever fitted a new shaft to a hammer you will realise what a fiddly job it is. A hammer head flying off its handle and around your workshop is not conducive to good working conditions.

6 Hammer

This tool is for making decorative lines as well as lines to follow for stitching and thonging. Try to buy one that opens to at least 2½cm (1in). A pair of dividers can be used for this job, but they are not as good.

7 Screw Crease

This is for bevelling the edges of your work, and makes it look clean and professional. They come in various sizes from 1–6. For belts and bags made from 2½ to 3½mm (about ⅛in) leather I would advise a number 3, although if you can afford it a 2 and a 4 are also handy to have.

8 Edge Shave

For making holes for stitching. Again these are available in sizes, so ask your dealer which size you will need for the thread and size of needle you are using. As these are fairly cheap buy more than one, as if you break one you may not be prepared to wait for a replacement to finish your project.

9 Awl

This tool is to mark the spacing for your stitching, i.e. 6 to the inch (or 25mm), 8 to the inch, and so on. Some have guides fitted to them so that you can keep your stitching at an exact distance from the edge. I use this type, and although it is expensive I think it is well worth it to keep your work looking neat and tidy. Nothing looks worse than a wiggly row of stitching. There are also cheap stitch-markers on the market, so try to make sure that the one you buy has angled wheel tips for correct stitching.

10 Stitch-marker

Here we refer to tools used for setting or punching holes and slits.

Punches and Setting Tools

You should find one with three teeth quite sufficient for making slits for thonging up your projects.

1 Thonging Chisel

This is used in conjuction with the three-pronged thonging chisel, and is good for corners and small areas which require thonging.

2 Single Thonging Chisel

Alternatively you can make one of these with a 6in (15cm) nail filed down and sawn flat.

3 Press-stud Setter These vary, as do the different types of press stud so, when ordering your press studs, buy a setting tool to fit. They are relatively inexpensive.

4 Wad Punch This is an oblong punch used for making slits to attach buckles on to belts and handbag straps; it is also useful for making watch-straps and wrist-bands. The length of the slit varies, and if you can, buy a couple of punches. 1½–2cm (about ¾in) are a good size with which to start.

5 Rawhide Mallet These are used in many trades, including leatherwork. Make sure the mallet you buy is not too heavy, as this will soon make your arms ache. If you are working on a carving, or making thonging slits on a large project, I would recommend you to use a small rawhide jeweller's mallet, as I have found the weight and head size are more suitable.

Fig. 2 Punching and setting tools: a three-teeth thonging chisel; b single thonging chisel; c press-stud setter; d wad punch; e rawhide mallet.

Fig. 3 Needles and thread.

Tools and materials that are essential for constructing as well as decorating your work.

Needles and Thread

Harness needles are undoubtedly the best. They have an oval eye and a blunt end. I would recommend either a number 2 or number 3 for a medium weight, and numbers 5 to 8 for cord thread.

Needles

You will need a piece of beeswax for waxing your thread to create better slip, and sealing your stitches. You can usually get this from a local candle-maker, or a candle-maker's supplier.

Wax

There are more than enough brands on the market in every country. The thickness of a thread is arrived at by counting the number of cords or strands that are twisted together to make it up. A 5- or 6-cord thread should be fine enough for most medium weight projects. Some thread is already waxed, but it is easy enough to run a length of untreated thread through your beeswax, which I feel is far more in keeping with the traditions of leather-work.

Thread

8

Thonging Needles   These are one of the few recent innovations which really help. They not only make thonging faster and easier, but also a lot neater. There are several types: the 'Life Eye Needle', the 'Hook and Eye Needle', and the 'Two Prong Needle', all of which are available from Tandy Tool Co. I suggest that as these are fairly cheap you can buy one of each, to find which suits you best.

Thonging Lace   Continuous thonging is by far the best for assembly, and many decorative braids. It can be bought in reels, spools, and short lengths, in different thicknesses – $\frac{3}{32}$in (2mm), $\frac{3}{16}$in (5mm), $\frac{3}{8}$in (9mm) etc. – depending on the job to be done.

Leather

When you first go to purchase leather from your supplier (some of whom are listed at the end of the book) you will be entering a new world, where a different language is used. Always ask the advice of your merchant; for instance, should you want to make a belt, say to the dealer that you want a piece of leather so thick – indicate with thumb and forefinger – so wide and so long. He will then advise you on the best type and piece for your requirements. Always ask the advice of your merchant, until you become more familiar with the material.

There are different ways of tanning leather for different purposes. *Oak Bark Tanned* has a hard finish for shoes, etc. *Vegetable Tanned* has a supple natural finish, most suitable for tooling; it is this type of leather which is most used by hand craftsmen. *Chrome* or *Semi-Chrome* tanned leather has a finish similar to vegetable tanned, soft, but with more body. This leather is mostly used for shoe uppers and garments. Most leather is sold in square feet, apart from shoe sole leather, which is sometimes sold by weight. The thickness is usually in millimetres. It is cheapest to buy the whole hide rather than selected pieces, but you will have to put up with things like the shoulder having heavier graining than the butt, or the belly being extra soft and fibrous, whereas the back will be nearly perfect in leather terms. I say nearly because leather, being a natural material, will always have small blemishes or even holes. Later, when you get to know your material better, you may decide to buy selected pieces (see Fig. 4), but for now stick with whole hides; or a good idea for beginners is to buy offcuts to practise on, as ruining good leather is an expensive business, as well as a terrible waste.

Cowhide   This is natural in colour, but can be bought pre-dyed. Its substance varies from 2mm to 8mm ($\frac{1}{8}$ to $\frac{3}{8}$in), and a hide will measure about 30 sq. ft. (280 sq. cm). The back and butt are the finest

9

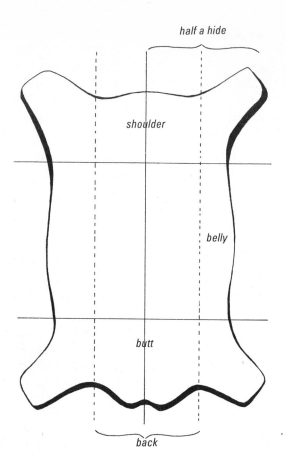

half a hide

shoulder

belly

butt

back

Fig. 4 Divisions of leather.

pieces of the hide, but all the leather can be used for most tooling, carving, and other craft projects. Vegetable tanned is the best, but chrome or semi-tanned may be used. You will find the latter more fibrous, though.

Calf

This is excellent leather, and can be used for carving, tooling, etc. In a thinner state it will also make beautiful garments. Its thickness varies from about $1\frac{1}{2}$ to 5mm ($\frac{1}{16}$ to $\frac{1}{4}$in), and a hide measures about 7 to 15 sq. ft (65 to 140 sq. cm).

Sheep

Nowhere near as good a quality as cow or calf. I would not advise tooling upon it, but it can be used for making nice plain belts, bags, hats, etc. It comes in a variety of colours as well as natural. It is mostly about $11\frac{1}{2}$mm ($\frac{1}{16}$ in) in thickness, and 6 to 14 sq. ft (55 to 130 sq. cm) in size.

Lining Leather

These leathers and suedes are used for lining to add a more luxurious finish to your work.

Skiver This is a very thin split sheepskin, ideal for lining. It is available in many colours, with a suede or leather finish. It is easy to work with.

Chrome Calf In its lightweight form this is a fine, smooth lining leather, again available in many colours.

Pigskin A thin pigskin as a lining finishes off an expensive project in just the right way.

Suede There are many kinds of suede in a variety of colours and finishes. It makes a soft, luxurious lining, and is also good for clothing, dresses, belts, and decorative appliqué work on bags, belts, jackets, etc.

Snake Skins

Although often expensive, these skins provide a particularly attractive decorative finish.

Indian Water Snake Also known as whip snake, these skins are excellent for belts or any decorative work on bags, hats or garments. They come in a large variety of colours and shades, and are also fairly inexpensive for the elegance they can add to many projects. Sizes are about 6in (15cm) wide tapering off, and about 4ft (120cm) long.

Python A very beautifully marked skin for making belts, bags and wallets. It also makes amazing decorative work. It is very expensive, and measures about 10in (2·5cm) wide tapering off, and up to 30ft (9m) long.

Alligator Makes beautiful wallets, bags, and even shoes. It comes in various shades of brown, and is very expensive. It is sold usually by the square centimetre, and skins are about 12ft (3·6m) wide and up to 5ft (150cm) long.

Remember, leather is the most important thing in your project apart from your hands, so when buying give yourself a good choice and make a careful selection, for you are trying to enhance the natural beauty of the leather, and not to disguise it.

These are the materials which give colour, sheen and gloss to your work.

Dyes, Glues and Finishes

Leather Dyes

Dyes are usually spirit or water based. There are many brand named ready-made dyes on the market, or you can make your own from the wide variety of colours available. I find spirit dyes the best to use, as they are more permanent and have better penetration into the leather; neither do they fade or run. If you wish to mix your own dyes you can do so by using aniline, a powder easily purchased from a French Polisher's supplier or a good D.I.Y. shop, mixed with methylated spirits until you achieve the colour you require. Then strain your mixture through a muslin bag into an airtight container, and there you have your dye ready to store. I would advise the beginner, however, to use a ready-made dye at first, as I consider the application of dye to be one of the hardest procedures of all, and by using a ready-made dye it will help you to acquire the feel you will need to be able to go on and mix your own. Buy your dyes in fairly large quantities, as this is far more economical. Always consult your supplier or craft shop about dyes, as you will be given advice on how to use the brand you buy. Dye manufacturers may be found in the List of Suppliers at the back of this book, many of whom will send you information about their products on request. You will need some small pieces of sponge or sheepskin for applying your dye and also some commercially-bought felt daubers for edge dyeing and small projects. A couple of old baking trays bought from an ironmonger, or even a jumble sale, are useful if you intend to use the dipping method of applying dye. Newspapers and even a plastic tablecloth are good for dyeing on, because if dye is spilt it will not come off any surface easily. A couple of children's paint-brushes are needed for dyeing in the background of carving, and also any small areas missed. Last, but not least, you will need a couple of pairs of rubber gloves (one for light colours and one for dark colours). You may think that this is too fussy for you, but leather is skin and so is the surface of your hands, and it is a massive job trying to remove dye from them. Many's the time my wife and I have been invited out, and I've had to shake hands, and even sit at table with light green hands; so be warned – it can be avoided.

Cleaners

Saddle soap, or a mixture of oxalic acid crystals (one teaspoon to one pint ($\frac{1}{2}$ litre) of cold water), both make ideal agents for cleaning your project before dyeing. This also helps dye penetration. Oxalic acid may be obtained from your chemist's shop, but be sure to tell your pharmacist what you require it for as he may have reservations in selling it to you. Just apply the oxalic acid mixture with a sponge, not too much, but sufficient to change the colour of the leather. Allow to dry before dyeing. With saddle soap, work it to a lather with a wet sponge, then apply it to the leather, rubbing in circular movements. Allow to dry, then rub it off with a dry cloth. Be careful not to appy too much, as this will leave a powdery white film on your project, and it will be hard to dye until the film is removed.

Finishes   When talking of a finish, I mean a lacquer or polish to give your project a nice sheen and shiny finish. Many craftsmen just prefer to polish their completed project with an aniline shoe cream of the appropriate colour, or a natural beeswax polish; alternatively you can also use a lacquer to give a harder shine. This is what I prefer to use. There are many to choose from, but you should experiment to find one to suit. 'Neat Lac' by Tandy, or 'Aquasheen' by Barrow Hepburn are both very good.

Glues   You will need some glue for attaching parts together for construction by sewing or lacing. It is handy to have two types of glue, a rubber solution for sticking in linings and light jobs such as suede work, and also a strong contact adhesive for holding the parts of your project together while you stitch or lace them. There are specialist leather glues such as 'Foss', but your dealer will recommend one for you, or you can use a domestic contact adhesive such as 'Evo-Stick'. You will also need a brush for applying glue, and some glue thinners. To keep your brushes clean it is a good idea to keep some thinners in large screw-top jars so that when you've finished with your brush you can keep it in a jar until you next require it.

Fittings   Fittings can add decoration to your work as well as serving a more obvious functional use.

Belt Buckles   These come in every shape and size imaginable, and are made of all types of materials – wood, leather, ivory, nickel, brass and silver. The longer you do leatherwork the more of an assortment of buckles you will collect. Buy buckles as you need them. They are sized by the inside width; in other words, the width of the leather that will fit them. I have listed buckle suppliers at the back of the book.

Eyelets   These are used for all manner of jobs; for fastening metal plates (e.g. key case fittings) and for reinforcing holes in a belt or strap. They come in all sizes, the larger ones being called grommets and

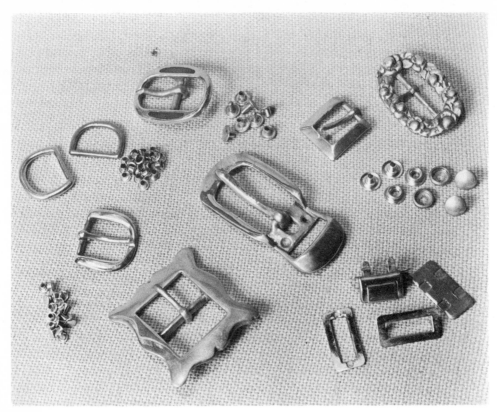

Fig. 5 A selection of fittings.

having a washer to hold the back more stable. They are fairly inexpensive, so you can afford to have a couple of sizes.

Tubular Rivets and Caps

These come in different lengths and head sizes, and are used for ornamental purposes, and for attaching parts together in the construction of handbags, belts, etc. They are available in brass and nickel finishes, and are very useful for attaching buckles to belts and straps. There is also a jewelled variety for decoration – these are called dots.

Press-studs

These have four parts, come in brass and nickel finishes, and vary in size. Make sure that the ones you buy are substantial, as they have many uses as leatherwork fastenings, and it is often awkward to fit new ones to a completed item without having to take it apart.

Dee Rings

It is always a good idea to keep a few dee rings and martingale rings for attaching handbag straps. Some ¾in (18mm) and 1in (25mm) ones will always be handy.

Locks   You will also need things such as turn-locks and snap-locks for catches on bags and pouches. It is best to buy these as they are needed, and often you will be able to make your own leather fastenings for handbags.

In this chapter I have tried to talk about the basic tools and materials, but I am by no means suggesting that you rush out and buy everything mentioned here, because it is not necessary. Later in the book when we talk about actual processes, and the use of individual tools, you will get more of an idea of what you want to start making, and what you will need to do it. I have not covered decorative tools in this chapter, as I did not want to confuse the issue. I intend to cover them at length later in the book in the sections on carving and tooling leather in Chapter 5; in the meantime, I suggest that we start with construction.

Getting to Work

2

In this chapter I intend to deal with the operations from designing and making a pattern to colouring or dyeing your work. Most of the operations here are relatively simple, but need a lot of practice to do well, and doing things well is the difference between being a craftsman and someone who is only dabbling in leatherwork.

Design

The subject of design constitutes a complete book on its own, but I shall deal with the elementaries here. Although I am covering it at this stage in the book, it is necessary to understand fully all the tools, materials and techniques before attempting to design your own projects. For the beginner, there are several specially designed projects in this book for you to make, and by cutting out the patterns and making the projects up for yourself you will learn the principles involved in designing your own work. I started like this, and a lot of my early work consisted of adaptations from other peoples' patterns until gradually I gained sufficient knowledge to make up my own designs. Even now, however, if I see an attractive mass-produced bag or belt, I may adapt its design to suit my own work and make it. Designing a new project is one of the most satisfying and rewarding parts of leatherwork, as most craftsmen will tell you, and is only pipped to the post by the satisfaction of seeing one of your own designs made up and finished off successfully, the way you visualised it. When you have mastered the techniques of leatherwork and are ready to start on your own designs, the first thing to do is to look about for ideas in books and magazines, shops, and even at leather goods belonging to friends. From these you will get an idea of what you want to make, and you can do some sketches of your designs. From the sketches you

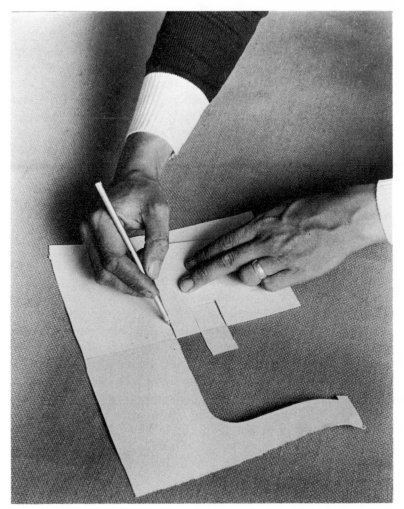

Fig. 6 Using the mirror image technique to copy one side from the other.

should then work out some rough dimensions, and how many separate parts will be needed for your project. For example, if you have designed a bag it will have a back, front, sides and a strap. You know then that you will need four pattern templates for your bag. If you should have to cut curves for bag flaps, etc. a good method is to fold in half a piece of paper of the size required, then draw your curve on one side until satisfied with the shape, then cut that half out – which will leave you a mirror image from which to copy the other side of your curve (see Fig. 6).

Note – always remember to allow for the thickness of your leather when making designs; also, make allowances for other things, such as bends, corners, and where pieces of leather overlap.

If you are designing for specific items such as knife sheaths, gun holsters and spectacle cases, it is best to design around the object by laying it on a piece of paper and then drawing around the item, allowing for the seams. You then have a shape that you know is the right size from which to start designing. Decorative designs such as carving, embossing and modelling, will be dealt with in a separate section later, but here we will cover basic things you need to know for overall designing. Many of the leatherworkers I know have become so interested in designing that not only do they design their own projects, but also design for other people, as I do myself.

When you have made your sketch, along with rough dimensions, you will be ready to start making your templates.

Making Pattern Templates

For anything you intend to make you will need pattern templates. These can be made of cardboard, hardboard, sheet tin, zinc, or galvanised iron, but if you only want to use a pattern a couple of times a stiff card should be quite adequate. The template is not just an aid to cutting out, but is also a way of checking that your ideas will work before you start making them up in leather which is expensive to replace if any mistakes have been made. By making your pattern you can then put the pieces together by sticking them with paper tape, or even stitching them together. You can then make sure that your project looks right – and if it doesn't you can adapt your pattern easily before transferring the design to the leather. Cardboard templates are easily made by using a pair of sharp scissors to cut out. The edges can then be reinforced with clear tape to stop wear. Your templates should be clearly marked, i.e. 'front', 'back', 'pockets' etc., so that after they have been stored away you know what's what.

More permanent templates can be made from sheet tin or zinc cut with a pair of snips, and then the edges filed smooth. Good templates should show all the holes and slots needed for press-studs, rivets, and so on; in fact all the fittings with which you intend to adorn the finished article. Although this takes up more time it is worth it as you will save a lot of time in the long run. When making a template for a belt or strap, or any item that is long and of uniform width, you need only make a pattern for the ends. Then you can mark one end, slide the pattern along your leather, measuring the distance between with a tape measure, and mark the other end with the same pattern (see Fig. 8).

When it comes to fitting your templates on to the leather to mark, make sure that you fit your patterns tightly together, so as to utilise space best. The grain on your pieces should all go the same way, usually across the hide. Use any blemished parts of the hide

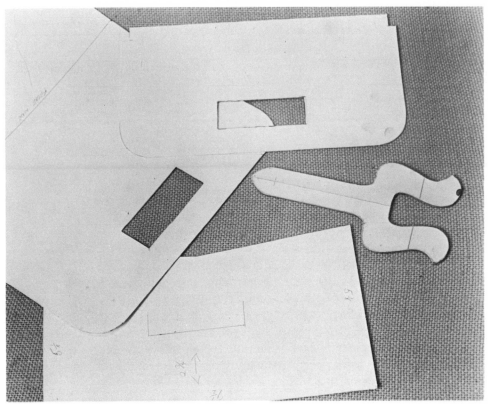

Fig. 7 Paper templates.

for pieces that will not be seen, such as under pockets, or for gussets. When marking round your templates use a pencil or an awl. Once your hide is marked up, you are ready to start. Always remember that the beauty and style of your finished project starts with the design, and the precision with which you have cut your templates, so time spent there is going to enhance your finished piece. This is the way in which all professional leather craftsmen work.

Cutting Out

Before starting, always make sure that your knife is sharp. Then cut along the straight lines you have marked from your pattern, using a steel ruler to cut against. Hold the knife squarely at an angle of about 45 degrees, and use enough pressure to go through your leather in one cut (see Fig. 9). When cutting a curved line for corners, etc. you can do this either freehand, or by making several straight cuts across your corner, gradually chipping the corner away. Practice at cutting curves will make perfect.

| 1 | 2 | 3 | 4 | 5 | 6 | 7 | 8 | 9 | 10 | 11 | 12 | 13 | 14 | tape measure | 85 | 86 | 87 | 88 | 89 | 90 | 91 | 92 | 93 | 94 | 95 | 96 | 97 | 98 | 99 |

template

leather

Fig. 8 Using belt template.

When cutting straps using a plough gauge, start by setting the sliding gauge to the width desired and then set the gauge to a straight edge on your leather, and push the whole knife up through your leather, cutting a perfect strap of uniform width. This can be repeated, cutting strap after strap. If you do not have a plough gauge and are cutting straps by knife, you will have to mark from the edge the width you require at intervals along the leather; then, using a long steel ruler or straight edge, cut along and slide the ruler up and cut again, until you are left with a strap. I used to cut belts and straps by this method for several years, and although tedious it works perfectly well. Only if you intend to make a lot of belts or straps does a plough gauge justify the investment.

Note: whichever way you cut straps, with a plough gauge or by hand, you will need a perfectly straight edge from which to work.

Fig. 9 Cutting corner.

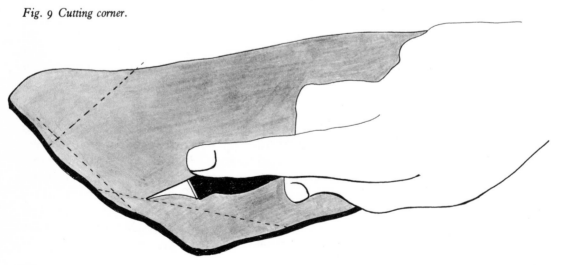

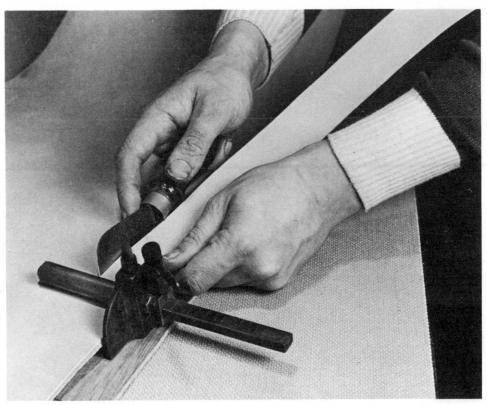

Fig. 10 Cutting belt strip using a plough gauge or strap cutter.

Creasing This is the process of putting lines for decoration or stitching along your project, using a screw crease. Open your screw crease up to the distance that you require from the edge, then case the leather (i.e. moisten lightly) and, using one blade of the screw crease against the edge, drag backwards around the leather, creasing a fairly deep and permanent line. If it is decorative work you may want to make a double line; in which case, open the screw crease a little wider and repeat the process. Creasing can also be done using a pair of dividers, by placing one point on the outside edge of the leather and using the other to mark the line. A plain project can look very attractive by just being double-creased.

Edge Bevelling This is bevelling the edges with an edge shave, which will bevel either the flesh or the grain side of the leather – or both in the case of belt edges and bag flaps. Edge shaves are numbered – the higher the number, the thicker the leather. As a rough guide, use the numbered edge crease that corresponds to the thickness of the leather being worked – i.e. use a number 3 edge shave on 3 to

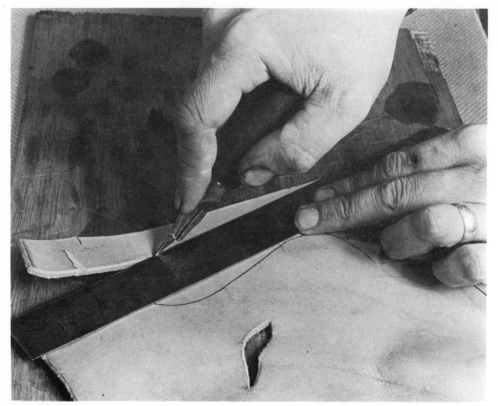

Fig. 11 Cutting out using straight edge.

3½mm (about ⅛in) leather. There are several different types of edge shave, but they all work by either pushing or pulling along the edge of the leather, thus taking off the corner edge, leaving it nicely rounded. Only edge the grain side of the leather where pieces are likely to be stitched together, but on flaps, etc. which are not being stitched or thonged edge both sides for a well-finished edge.

Skiving

This is the technique of shaving or thinning leather down for folding, or where there are several layers to be stitched or thonged together, and you do not wish to end up with a thick edge. There are several tools available for this, including a type of safety skiver which uses razor blades, but I would recommend either a proper skiving knife bought from one of the saddlers' tool suppliers, or a skirt shave. Both tools are used in the same way. Keeping your fingers pointing down towards the blade, shave off the leather with a series of forward thrusts from the forearm, making sure that the angle of your blade is not too acute as this will tend to hack up your leather. One of the most important points is to have skiving tools

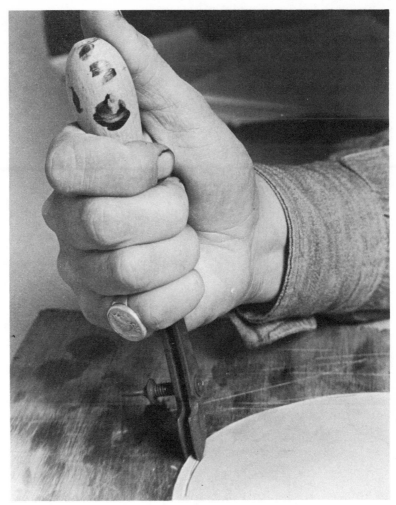

Fig. 12 Creasing.

razor sharp. If you are fixing several pieces of leather together, such as attaching a pocket, you will need to skive the edges of the leather only enough to reduce their combined thicknesses to approximately that of a single piece of the original thickness. Where you are attaching belt and strap buckles you will only need to thin sufficiently to fold neatly over the buckle bar. Although I have dealt with skiving at this stage, in some cases you will not use it until after your project is dyed, but the technique remains the same.

Punching Holes You will find various types of punches for making holes for press-studs and for making slits for buckles, but the six-way punch plier is by far the most common, and versatile. When using

23

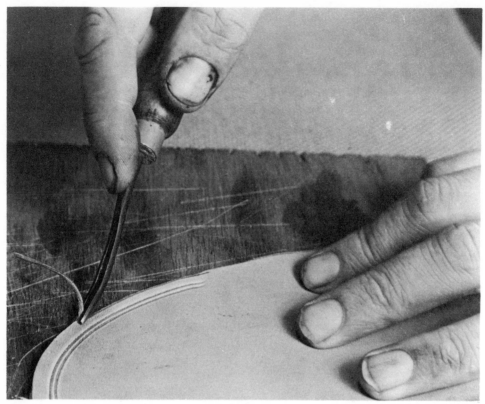

Fig. 13 Edge bevelling.

the six-way punch plier you simply turn the revolving chamber until the particular sized punch tube you require is opposite the anvil; then, making sure that the tube is central to the mark showing where you want the hole, squeeze the plier together to make a nice clean cut, having also made sure that you are not punching more layers than required.

You will find that you cannot reach very far from the edge of the leather with the punch plier because of the tool's small throat, so you may need to use either a single round punch instead, or modify your use of the six-way punch. The single round drive punch is used by placing the leather flat on a piece of wood or thick leather, then striking the back of the punch squarely with a mallet. The punch must be kept vertical in order to make a clean cut. To use the six-way punch, select the punch required by turning the chamber until it is opposite its normal punching position against the anvil; then, squeezing the plier closed, position the tube on the mark and strike the back of the anvil with your mallet (see Fig. 16).

24

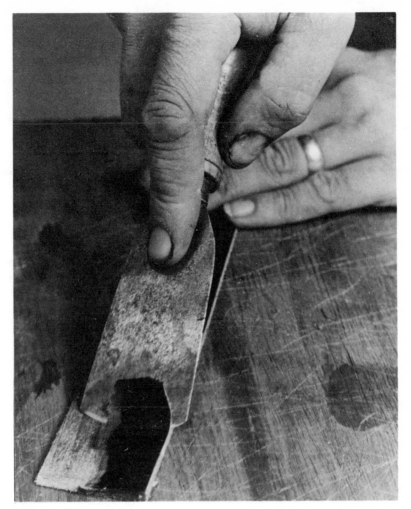

Fig. 14 Skiving.

A crew punch is designed to make an oblong hole for attaching buckles and making holes in bag gussets to attach straps. It is used in the same way as the round drive punch. Place the leather flat on a piece of wood, then place the cutting end of the punch in the middle of the mark made for the hole. Strike firmly with your mallet. An illustration of a crew punch appears in the photostrip for making a belt (Stage 7) on p. 67. Alternatively, slits can be made using your six-way punch plier. First mark out your slit, then punch a hole of the correct width at each end of the slit. With a knife cut down the line from one hole to the other on both sides, thus freeing the piece in the middle and forming your slit (see Fig. 17).

You can use a single drive punch of the correct hole size for this

Fig. 15 Ordinary way of using a six-way punch plier.

method, but to build up a collection of drive punches is far more expensive than buying one decent six-way punch plier. Also you will find the punch plier much more versatile as I have already shown.

The oval punch is used for making holes for belt and strap fastenings, and is used in the same way as the round drive and crew punches. There is also a single punch plier for which you can buy a gauge in order to space holes evenly for thonging and lacing (the processes in which the single punch is used). Once again, however, you can use 'old faithful' – the six-way punch plier. Using your screw crease to make a line a set distance from the edge of the leather, you then set a pair of dividers to the spacing you require between the holes, and walk the points along the line. Now centre the punch over each mark, and you will have perfectly spaced lacing holes.

There are also strap end punches, which come in either half-round or pointed designs, and are used for cutting strap and belt ends neatly, although this job may be easily done by knife.

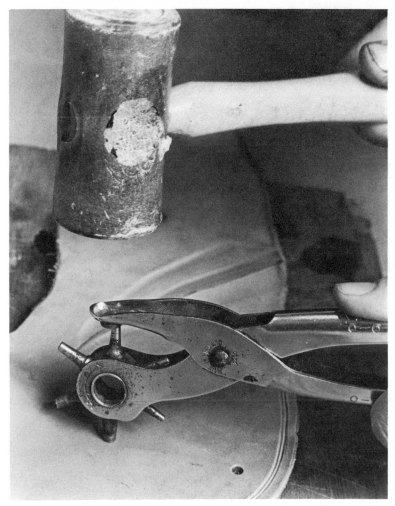

Fig. 16 Alternative way of using a six-way punch plier.

Should you wish to make round leather buttons, you can also buy washer cutting punches, which are larger versions of a round drive punch. These can also be used for making patterns. With all single drive type punches never use a steel hammer, as this will damage your punches by bevelling, splaying and bending them. A good leathercraftsman always respects his or another's tools, as he knows that without them he cannot make a living.

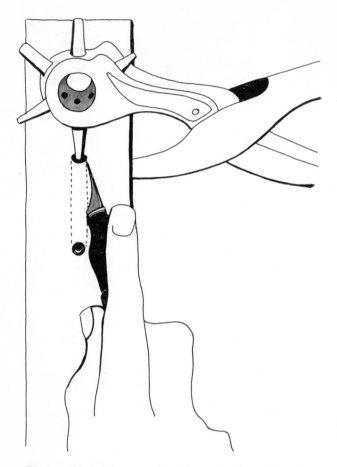

Fig. 17 *Alternative way of making a slit. You will see I have taken out a hole of the correct size at each end of my slit using a six-way punch plier, and with a knife I am cutting through on either side in a straight line to free the middle piece of leather, thus forming a nice neat slit round the holes at each end.*

3   Leather Colouring

A piece of natural leather is fertile ground on which to let your imagination run riot. Although at first you will probably make things up in natural leather, you will eventually want to enter into colouring leather or dyeing it. Dyeing is one of the most difficult techniques to master, as most leatherworkers will tell you. It took me a long time to master, before I started getting the colours I wanted, and only after a lot of patient experimenting with different brands and mixtures could I achieve the rich tones I desired.

Before you dye your project you will normally have creased, edged, and put what decoration you require (carving, embossing, etc.) on your project, but not assembled it. You can then dye all the individual parts of the project thoroughly before it is made up. If you dye after assembly, there may be areas which are hard to reach; also you may wish to stitch or thong in a contrasting colour, or even make your project up in 'two-tone'. There are leatherworkers who dye projects after assembling them, but this means they are limited to one-colour dyeing.

Before you start to dye your project, cover your bench with some old newspapers, or a plastic tablecloth. Newspaper is best because it will absorb any surplus dye from your leather. Make sure all your tools and leather are well clear of the dyeing area, and not within splashing distance. It may seem as though I am stating the obvious here, but I can remember being so eager to get a new project finished on one occasion that I didn't bother to clear a space to work in. At the time I was working in the lounge, so while dyeing my project I also splash-dyed the carpet and furniture, which I then had to replace, making that particular bag very expensive indeed!

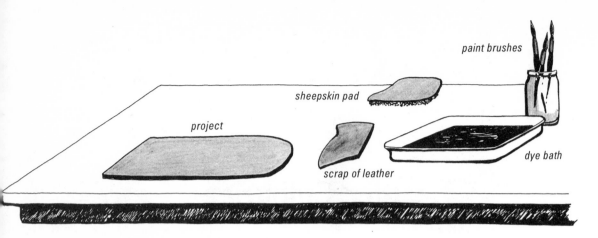

Fig. 18 Laying out your bench ready for dyeing.

So, having cleared sufficient space and covered your bench, you now need to make sure that your leather is clean and free from dust, grease, glue spots and any tallow residue left from the tanning process. You can do this by cleaning (see Chapter 1, *Cleaners*). When your project is clean and dry, you are ready to commence. Always experiment with a piece of scrap leather first, as you do not want to make a mistake at this point. There are numerous ways of applying different dyes.

Water Dyes

These are best applied with a brush, using long, even strokes. Apply several coats, going in different directions in order to avoid streaks. Always allow each coat to dry thoroughly, as the colour differs when wet. You should always use a varnish or lacquer over water-based dyes to prevent the dye from running, or coming off if it gets wet.

Another method is to dip-dye your project. This is a good method for belts and items where you need to colour the back as well as the front. You will need a fairly large baking tray for this. Half fill with your dye, then run the leather through the dye and on to the newspaper-covered bench, with the grain facing upwards. Then, with a sponge or a piece of sheepskin, remove the dye residue by rubbing backwards and forwards across the leather a couple of times. If the leather is more square, make circular strokes, spreading the colour evenly. Experiment for yourself with the dyes on scrap leather, as there are numerous ways of applying dye, and you will find a particular method which suits you.

30

Fig. 19 Application of water dye.

Spirit Dyes This is the type of dye which I work with most often (as do most of the leatherworkers I know), as it gives far more permanent and rich tones. Spirit dyes can be applied in the same way as water dyes. When applying the dye, place your piece of leather on the newspaper in the centre of your bench, and have your dye at hand in a small dish. Then, with a piece of sponge or sheepskin, or a felt dauber, dip into the dye and apply to the leather in fairly swift, circular movements until your colour is evenly spread. Repeat, building up the coats until the right depth of colour is achieved. Before you put your dye back into its bottle, make sure that your leather dries to the colour required, as invariably it will dry lighter than expected. When you have sufficient experience, you will learn to judge how a colour, when wet, will dry out.

Dip-dyeing with spirit dyes is done by exactly the same method as with water dyes. You will need to dye the backs of belts and handbag flaps, and other pieces that are visible when your project is assembled. I prefer to dye the backs of all my work, as I think it gives a more professional finish. Nothing looks worse, to my mind, than seeing a natural belt-back with a couple of splodges of dye on it.

Much of the dye on the market carries its own instructions for application. Again, experimenting for yourself, using the guides I have mentioned, will reward you with experience in dyeing.

Fig. 20 Application of spirit dye.

Acrylic Paint and Enamels

These can be used for colouring leather where a bright colour is required, and even for painting pictures on leather. They have little or no penetration, and more or less just lie on the surface of the leather. Application should be with a camel-hair brush, which will need cleaning after every use. Since they lie only on the surface of the leather, these colours will need protecting in order to prevent their wearing or rubbing off. Their best use is for painting in depressed patterns.

Dyeing Black   Black is undoubtedly one of the most problematic and frustrating colours to dye, as it is difficult to obtain a deep and lasting colour without it streaking or fading to a light grey. However, as black is the darkest colour you can dye, it can often be used to cover a bad dye job of a lighter colour. Where you are limited in the number of coats you can apply, water-based black dye is the easier to use, but its colour is not as strong or lasting as that of a solvent or spirit-based dye. As a general rule, solvent or spirit-based dyes have far better penetration and their colours are more lasting. With black dyes of many brands the problem seems to be that the solvent or spirit evaporates if the dye is kept for any length of time, so that when it is applied to the leather it dries leaving a powdery metallic sheen on the surface. In more severe cases this can be rubbed off, but leaves areas of leather undyed. This problem can be avoided by topping up your black dye with a little methylated spirits. When dyeing black, however, it is best to follow a few simple rules in order to achieve a permanent, lasting colour, which will not fade or rub off on hands and clothes.

Firstly, your leather needs to be clean and dry. This can be done with an oxalic acid solution (see Chapter 1, *Cleaners*), or with a little half-diluted ammonia, which should be rubbed across the surface of the leather. When completely dry, apply black dye with a sheepskin pad or a sponge, using lots of newspaper to absorb any excess dye. You should also wear a pair of rubber gloves to protect your hands – black dye has a tendency to go everywhere if you are not careful. Never use the same piece of sheepskin or sponge for another project after it has dried as dry dye tends to go powdery and leaves an excess residue on your leather. So, always use a clean pad for every project.

After having applied one coat and allowed it to dry, rub off any powder residue with a dry rag. Then apply a second coat a little more liberally, working your dye into the leather. Allow to dry fully, then polish up with a dry cloth before applying a finishing lacquer to your project. If the colour is still not satisfactory, you should try applying a first coat of another colour (brown, blue, etc.) before the two coats of black. As you need to apply a lot of black dye to leather it tends to dry out the natural oils, so these will need replacing to prevent the leather from cracking. This can be done with many of the skin food creams on the market – 'Lexol', 'Ko-Cho-Line', 'Carnauba Cream', and so on; also with saddle soap. Neatsfoot oil is recommended for thicker leather as it will really penetrate. All of these should be applied and then allowed to dry into the leather overnight, before you apply your finishing lacquer.

By following these few tips you should end up with a good black dye job, and as I said earlier, if you make a mess of dyeing something another colour, you can always dye it black.

These come in several forms – paste, liquid, and water soluble. **Antique Finishes**
Their function is to two-tone and add light and shade to carved
and embossed, as well as plain dyed, leather and to enhance its
appearance. There are too many different makes to list here, but
two which I have found satisfactory are 'Barrow Hepburn Antique
Finish', and 'Fiebings Antique Finish'. They come in different
colours, and you should use the same colour antique as your dye –
tan for tan, and so on. They are all applied in roughly the same
way, but always follow the manufacturer's instructions for best
results, as each make may differ slightly.

Apply the antique liberally with a dry brush, working well into
any carved or embossed areas. Then wipe off the excess, leaving
the antique in any impressions and a thin coat on the surface of the
leather. Allow to dry, then polish up with a dry cloth before
applying the finishing lacquer. Antiques are always used over dye,
never (as a rule) on natural leather, as they are not a dye, only a
highlighter. They will bring out the grain of your leather beautifully, and enhance any carving or embossing on your projects.

Fig. 21 Dyeing embossing.

Dyeing Embossing

When you want to multi-colour dye embossing, to build up a colourful pattern, you should always start with the lightest colour first, building up gradually. To start with, make up a rubber with which to apply the dye, using a piece of soft material (a piece of old tee-shirt is ideal) wrapped round a piece of cotton wool. Dip this into your dye – which should be contained in a small bowl – and dab off any excess on to a piece of newspaper, making a flat surface on your rubber. Wipe over the leather with even strokes. You will find that the embossed impressions will not take colour, but the surface of the leather will. Now you can colour in the embossed areas with different colours, applying them with a small brush, gradually building up your design.

Blocking-off Dye

This is the method used for leaving some parts of the leather natural and dyeing others. It can be done in two ways; one is by using a clear lacquer applied over the area which you wish to remain natural. Using a brush, apply two coats, and make sure you have covered it completely. When the lacquer is dry you can dye the rest, leaving the blocked-off area natural. The other method is to dip a brush into hot beeswax and apply a couple of coats to the area you wish to remain natural. When the wax is dry you can then dye the rest of the project to achieve the effect required. There are many effects that can be achieved with this method. You can also combine the various techniques – for example, you could have a carved bag in dark brown with an antique finish, with the owner's initials blocked off in natural. I am sure that with a bit of experimenting you will find lots of ways in which to use this technique.

Dyeing Carving

When talking of dyeing carving, I really mean dyeing the background of the carving, as your project's overall colouring should have been achieved using the methods previously described, with spirit or water dyes, unless of course your project is to be natural, or have natural coloured carving.

There are two types of carving; a carving which is framed around and then completely backgrounded in with a stippled effect, or open background carving. The latter is when you have a small carved section with a wide open border. You will be more familiar with these after reading the section on carving.

Dealing firstly with a framed carving background: for this you will need your fine sable artist's brush and your dye of contrasting colour (in a small bottle). Load your brush with dye, touch it on to a piece of scrap leather to check the colour and remove excess dye.

Now, holding the brush straight, touch it on to the stippled background of the leather and colour in until the background is evenly coloured and contrasts nicely with the carving. It is useful to have a piece of clean paper with which to cover one part of the carving while dyeing in the other. Start dyeing at the edge of the carving, and work towards the middle. The colour should not spread or bleed on to the raised area of the carving. If this happens it is usually due to having too much dye on your brush.

When dyeing an open background, or a design without a border line, begin by dyeing in the background in the middle of your carving, using the method described above. Then dye round the raised edges of your design with a fine brush to within about 1in (25mm) all round. Apply a couple of coats. Now you are ready to dye in the uncarved area. This you can do with a felt dauber, or larger brush. Apply at least two good coats. The main thing to remember when dyeing the background of carving is to take your time, and be careful not to bleed dye up or on to the raised edges of your design.

Fig. 22 Dyeing in background to framed carving.

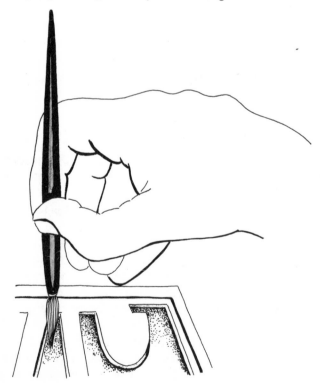

Fig. 23 Open background dyeing.

Edge Dyeing

Edge dyeing is not necessary on projects that have been dip-dyed, but where the grain and the flesh side of the leather have been dyed separately, leaving a raw edge exposed, this edge will need to be dyed. It is these finishing touches, such as edge dyeing and bevelling, which add 'class' to your leatherwork. Burnishing edges will be dealt with later in the section on finishing your project.

For dyeing, firstly you will need an applicator. This can be a brush, or felt dauber, or you can make applicators with a piece of felt about 3mm ($\frac{1}{8}$in) thick held in a clothes peg. Alternatively, you can buy a felt marker from a stationer's, making sure it has a wide felt tip. Cut a vee groove into the tip, empty out the ink and replace it with leather dye. This makes a very neat applicator. Place your project on a bench so that the edge to be dyed overlaps. This makes it easy to apply the dye evenly all round the edges of your project.

Edges are usually dyed in black, but there is no hard and fast rule.

Applying Clear Lacquer and Protective Finishes

These are applied to preserve and protect your projects, and they consist of lacquers such as 'Neat-Lac', and 'Aqua-Sheen', to mention only two of the many which are available on the market. Lacquers give a hard shine to your leather. They have no colour, so can be used on natural as well as dyed leathers. They are applied

37

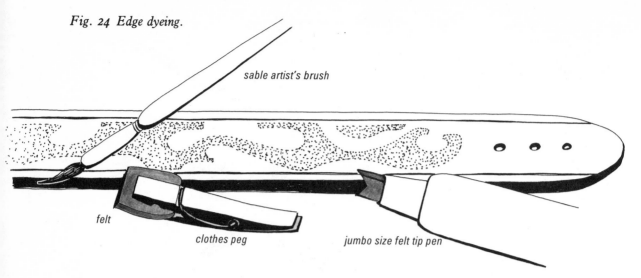

Fig. 24 Edge dyeing.

sable artist's brush

felt

clothes peg

jumbo size felt tip pen

after antique finishes and all other colouring is dry, and can be applied either before or after assembly. I find that applying them before protects from accidental markings while you are assembling your project.

Special leather lacquers do not crack or come off, so projects are permanently protected from the elements of heat and atmosphere which cause leather to deteriorate. Other types of protective finishes are oils and polishes, such as 'Neatsfoot Oil', 'Lexol', and 'Ko-Cho-Line'. These also give a more natural look to your projects, although they require more work to rub into the leather, and in many cases need to be left to soak in. You can use these lubricants in conjunction with lacquer (see the section on *Dyeing Black* for technique). All finishes, whether cream, lacquer, polishes or oils, should carry instructions for use, but most applications can be made by using a rubber of soft material wrapped around cotton wool, or a sponge, brush, or sheepskin pad. Lacquers are generally quicker to apply and dry than oils and creams, which require a fair amount of elbow grease to work into the leather. Always remember, the time you put into these processes will show in your finished project.

4 Methods of Assembling Your Work

Assembling your projects – this is where the imagination and forethought of your ideas come to life, and where the patient preparation of pattern templates and operations up to dyeing should pay dividends. Your project should now be dyed, lacquered, and ready to put together.

Glueing Projects such as bags, hats and purses will need to be glued together in order to hold one part to another and enable you to stitch or thong them more easily. I would recommend a contact adhesive such as 'Evo-Stik' or 'Foss' (green tin), a specialist leather glue, for heavier cowhide projects. For light leathers such as calf or suede, and for attaching linings, a rubber solution such as 'Copydex' will suffice. You will need a good glue brush and a jar of thinners recommended for the type of glue you are using. After each glueing job return your brush to a jar which is about one-third filled with thinners (or just above bristle height). This will prolong the life of your brush, and make it easier to apply the glue.

When using contact adhesive, apply a thin coat to each of the pieces you intend to stick together, and allow to dry until you can touch the surface without getting glue on your fingers. Then firmly hold the parts together for a couple of minutes, until securely bonded. If you are only glueing a seam on a bag, for instance, you will need only about a $\frac{1}{2}$ in (12mm) wide line of glue along each piece of the leather edges which you intend to sew together.

When you want to attach pieces of leather to each other, grain to grain, you will find that where you have dyed and lacquered the leather will not stick properly, as the glue will not adhere to the smooth surface. You will need firstly to place the smaller of the two pieces over the other, where they are to be attached. Then mark round the outline with a soft pencil. You then score the pieces with a sharp knife point, making several criss-cross scratches within the outline. This creates a surface to which the glue will adhere and form a good bond.

Glueing Together
Thong and Lace

If you are to lace a long project, there will come a time when you need to splice two pieces of lace together. To do this, you will need to skive off the two ends of the lace to a slope, one on the grain side of one lace, and the other on the flesh side of the other lace. Spread a thin layer of glue on each slope, and allow to dry. Then push them firmly together, so that you have a continuous piece of lace.

Fig. 25 Skiving lace for glueing together.

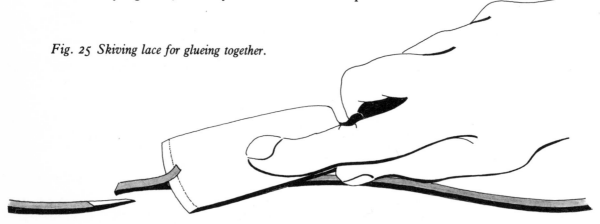

Glueing in a Lining

When lining a project, lay out all the separate pieces to be lined, and all your lining material. You can then use the individual leather parts as patterns for lining. When you have all the parts marked off on the lining, cut round about 1in (25mm) wide of the line. Then spread some rubber solution on to the flesh side of your leather, and attach the lining at one end while holding the other end clear. Gradually smooth along the lining, until the complete piece is in place. Allow to dry for a couple of minutes, then with a pair of scissors trim off any excess lining. You are then ready to assemble the project. Where the leather is to be bent, such as with a bag or purse flap, smooth the lining up to the bend, make the bend, and then smooth the rest of the lining into place.

40

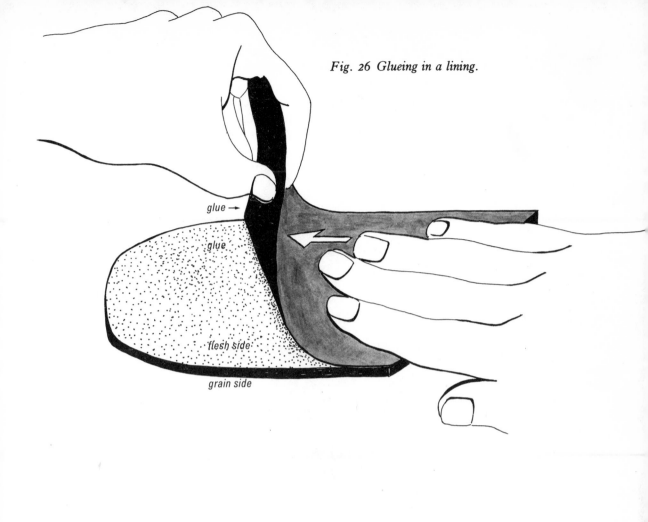

Fig. 26 Glueing in a lining.

glue →

glue

flesh side

grain side

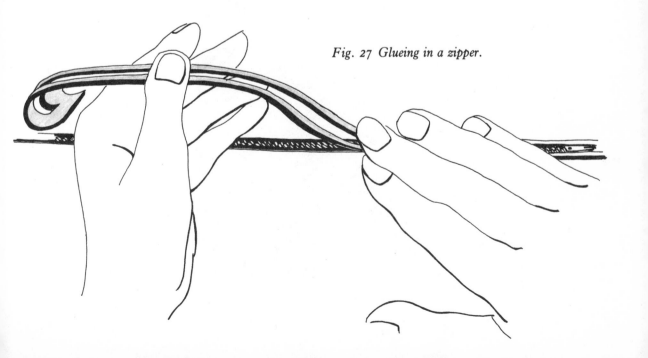

Fig. 27 Glueing in a zipper.

When you need to glue in a zipper ready for stitching, apply glue *Glueing in a Zipper*
to the cloth edges of the zipper and also along the flesh side of the
edges of the zipper opening. Now, starting with the tag end of the
zipper, smooth the cloth edges on to the flesh side of the leather
edges along the length of the zipper, until it is firmly in place.
Make sure that the opening is of uniform width all the way along,
and that the zip itself is not sticking. You are now ready to sew the
zipper in place.

Although there are many different types of stitches which may be **Stitching**
used on leather, including the numerous traditional needlework
stitches such as running stitch and blanket stitch, there is really
only one proper way to stitch leather. That is with the saddler's
stitch, and this is the only stitch I intend to deal with in this
section.

Fig. 28 Using a stitch marker to make marks ready for stitching.

In spite of saddle stitch being a little more difficult than others, I believe that if you start with this one and gradually master it, the appearance of your work will be greatly improved, and you will also have the satisfaction of knowing that you are working in the traditional way handed down over many hundreds of years.

When beginning to stitch, start by marking your stitches along your ready-made crease (see Chapter 2, *Creasing*). This you will do with a stitch-marker. The number of stitches per inch will vary, but on most projects to begin with somewhere between six to eight stitches per inch (or 25mm) should be sufficient. On small light-weight leather projects you can use as many as twelve stitches to the inch, using a finer needle and thread than normal. Some of the stitch-markers (such as the one I am using in Fig. 28 from Blanchard, Paris) are made in such a way that you can change wheels for different numbers of stitches per inch, but even with a single fixed-wheel stitch-marker you can vary the number of stitches by only stitching every other mark, or every other two marks, and so on, until the desired number of stitches is achieved.

Fig. 29 Threading a needle using locking stitch. The arrows indicate direction of thread.

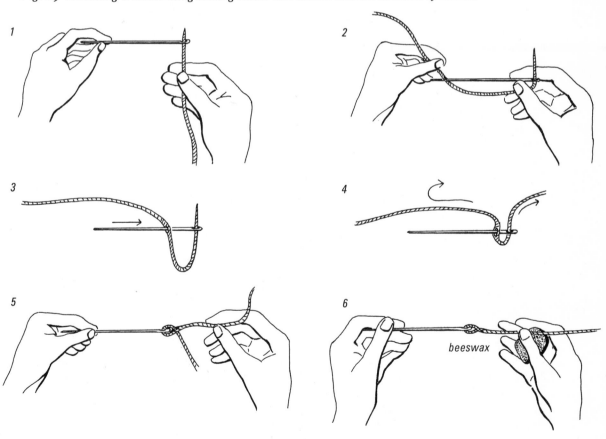

When marking your stitches, push your stitch-marking wheel along the crease line, which should be about a ¼in (6mm) from the edge of your leather. This will then leave a series of marks by which you can make a uniform stitch. Once your pieces of leather are marked, they can be glued together. *Note* – you only need to mark the front piece of leather.

You are now ready to start sewing; you will need a diamond shaped awl, two egg-eyed harness needles (size number 2 or 3), 5- or 6-cord linen thread, and a block of beeswax. Further details of these can be found in Chapter 2, *Needles and Thread*.

Now cut a length of thread, which should be no longer than the length of your arms when extended. The thread should now be pulled through the block of beeswax, creating enough friction to make the wax penetrate the thread. The ends of the thread will need to be scraped with the edge of a knife, tapering them to a point, and then rewaxed.

Now thread your needles, using a locking knot to keep the thread from coming away from the needle. This is achieved by following stages 1 to 6 in Fig. 29. With the awl stab through the first stitch mark at the correct angle left by your stitch marker, then push the needle through, leaving half the thread on one side, and half on the other. Now stab a second hole, and pass both needles through together in opposite directions, like crossed swords. Always insert the needles in the same order; the right-hand needle through the top of the hole, the left through the bottom. As you pull the thread together you will be left with two loops. Drop each needle through the loop left by the other needle, and then pull tight, thus locking off every stitch. Continue along in this way until your line of stitching is complete. To finish stitching, reverse-stitch three or four holes, then cut the thread off close to the leather, leaving no straggly ends. Always remember when making holes, keep the awl level, as you do not want your stitching lower or higher at the back than it is at the front. When stitching is complete, tap along it with the heel of a hammer so as to set (push down) the stitches.

If the surface stitches of seams are likely to be subjected to wear, it will be necessary to make a small groove or channel in which to recess the stitching. This can be done with a tool called a race, or groover, which when dragged along the crease line of the leather will make a small channel in which the stitches will lie and be protected.

A handy stitching aid to have is a stitching clamp, or pony. This will hold your leather securely in place while you are stitching, allowing you to have both hands free. It is made from two sections of barrel sprung together, so that at the top you have a jaw to hold the work, while lower down where the staves bow out sufficient room is left for large projects such as bags and so on. Stitching

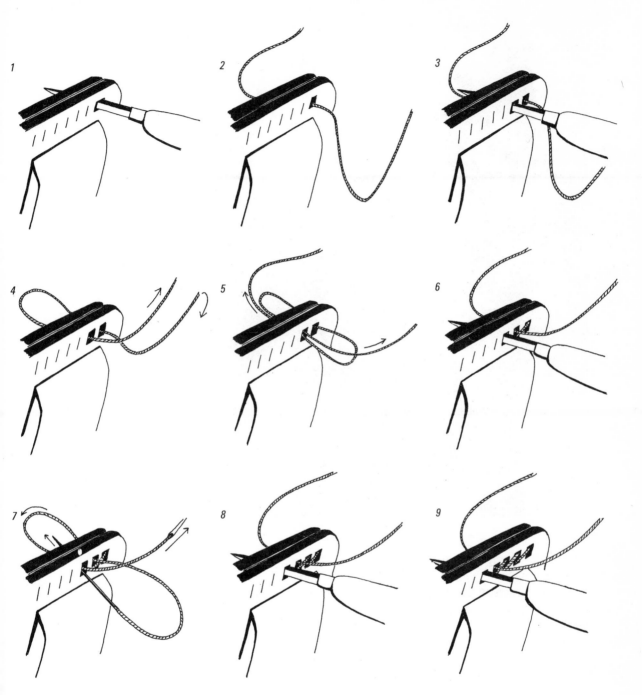

Fig. 30 Saddle stitching using two needles. The arrows indicate direction of thread.

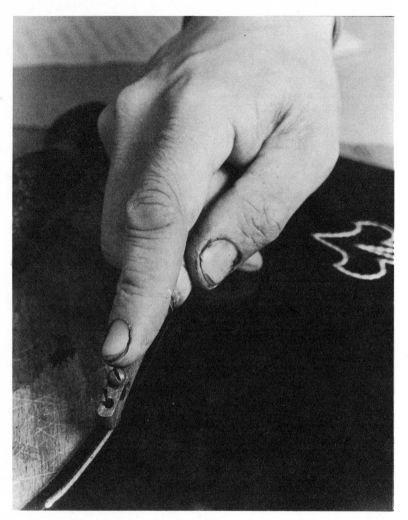

Fig. 31 Making a groove for stitching.

ponies and clamps can sometimes be bought cheaply in second-hand shops, but there are some modern versions available from companies such as the Tandy Leather Co. If you should know a cooper (barrel-maker) you could always have one made, as these were the people who made them for leathercraftsmen of the past. Failing this, you could always make one yourself from an old barrel or the tops of two curved chairbacks. Whichever way you acquire one, they really are most useful things to have, and will make stitching much easier.

Saddle stitching takes a long time to become proficient at, but the man who taught me didn't even have to look down at the work. You would simply see his hands fly apart and together (reminiscent of a sea lion!). He would stitch at a remarkable speed. When I met him he was in his fifties, and had been making boots by hand since the age of thirteen at his home in Cyprus. When he first

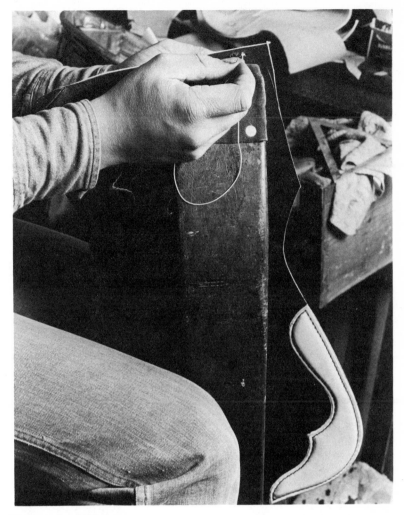

Fig. 32 A stitching pony.

started stitching he used pig bristles as needles; when the ends were split, thread could be attached to them. He also made his own thread, by pulling out five or six lengths of hemp line and then moistening them, and twisting them together by rolling them with the palm of his hand on his knee. Finally he pulled them through the wax to bind them together, thus creating a 5- or 6-twist thread. The last time I saw him was when I left London some ten years ago, where he was working making boots for some of the top show business and sports personalities throughout the world. The most valuable advice which he gave me on stitching, and which I will pass on to you, was this: always stitch slowly and carefully at first, making sure that the stitches are right. Gradually the speed will come on its own.

Saddle stitching is extremely hard on the hands, as the thread begins to cut into your fingers when you are doing a lot of sewing.

Many people make themselves little leather rings, or wear sticking plasters wrapped around their fingers, or even use a saddler's palm to enable them to push the needle through more easily. Personally I have always found all these things an encumbrance to work with, as your hands and fingers will harden up naturally in time. But this is something best left to you, and whichever you find the easiest.

Always stitch towards you, as when stitching away on a large project you are inclined to over-reach. There are many nice contrasts which can be made between your thread and leather colours; dark brown leather looks good stitched in drab (a fawny white colour) thread, or even yellow, and tan or natural leather looks well when stitched in brown or black. I shall deal with this point further in the section on decorative stitching, but experiments with contrasting threads are worth exploring for yourself.

Thonging, Lacing or Braiding

These all refer to the same thing. Using lace or thong for decoration or construction decoration will be discussed later, but here I intend to deal with making a seam for construction with thong, as opposed to other methods of construction such as sewing.

There are several ways of thonging, from the simple whip lace to the more difficult Spanish edge lacings, and all require varying amounts of skill and practice. For thonging you will need a reel of thong in the width required – ⅛in (3mm), etc. – a multiple and a single thonging chisel, a thonging needle and a thonging awl.

Whipstitch

This is the simplest method of thonging. Firstly you will need to make thonging slits along the crease line on the edge of the leather where the seam is to be made. Lay your project on a flat pounding block, then put the points of the chisel to your leather. Now, holding the chisel straight, punch through the leather by striking the back of the chisel with a mallet (do not use a hammer, as this will damage your chisel). When you have made the first slits, you

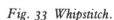

Fig. 33 Whipstitch.

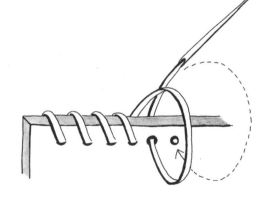

48

then insert the first tooth of your chisel in the last slit you made, and drive through again. Repeat until all the slits are made for corners, and more inaccessible places. Use the single prong chisel in the same way. You can also use your six-way punch plier for making holes for thonging, having marked your spacing with a pair of dividers stepped along the crease line, or even with a spacing gauge made to fit some makes of punch plier. Personally I use a pair of ordinary non-revolving punch pliers, which I got a friend to adapt by welding two prongs $\frac{1}{8}$in (3mm) wide and $\frac{1}{8}$in (3mm) apart, thus making me a handy thonging slit punch. If you know someone who works in a garage, or has access to welding gear, they will find this quite a simple job to do for you.

When all your slits are made, you then need to cut a length of thong measuring roughly 1m (3ft). Attach a thonging needle to one end, and pass through the first slit, securing the loose end with

Fig. 34 Making thonging slits, using a three-teeth thonging chisel.

a little glue. Then sew over the first hole and into the second, and so on. When working round corners, you will find it necessary to go through the same hole twice on each side of the corner, splicing the thong when needed (see the section on *Glueing* p. 39). If your slits are too tight, they can be opened up with a thonging awl. When reaching the end, pull the thong through three or four stitches on the back of your seam, and glue down securely. Always hold the project with the front towards you, and work from the front to the back.

This is a lacing often used for book covers and handbags. It is done in a similar way to whipstitch lacing, but through holes instead of slits, and using a wide lace ($\frac{1}{4}$in or 6mm) through a smallish hole, to create an effect of the thong splaying out on the edge. Firstly mark your holes, using a pair of dividers stepped along the crease line on the edge of your leather, or using a punch gauge. Make your holes the same distance apart as the width of the lace; then, having cut a point on the end of your lace, go through the first hole holding the front of the project towards you, and working from front to back. Then go over the edge into the second hole, and so on. When tackling corners you may need to go through the same hole several times, to cover the edge fully. When finishing, take the point back through a couple of stitches on the reverse side of the project, glue down to secure, and trim off. You may need to vary the width of the holes from the edge of the leather to achieve the right look and flow to your lacing, so start by experimenting with a piece of scrap leather.

Florentine Lacing

Fig. 35 Florentine lacing.

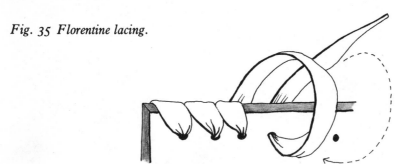

This is a really durable and decorative way of assembling projects such as bags and cases, especially if you are lining them. The amount of thong needed should be about five or six times the length of the area to be thonged, remembering to use it in lengths of about a metre or 3ft at a time. Longer lengths tend to fray with the wear of constantly being pulled through the slits, as well as becoming extremely entangled!

Spanish Edge Lacing of Two Loops

Fig. 36 Spanish edge lacing.

After having made your thonging slits and attaching a lacing needle to your thong, start (following Fig. 36), with the front of the project towards you, by taking your thong through the first slit, from the front, over the edge of the leather and into the second slit (1), thus forming a cross on the edge of the leather. Then take the thong over the edge and under the cross formed by the other two thongs (2), and pull to tighten. Now take the thong through the third slit (3), forming a second cross, then over the edge and under the second cross (4), and tighten. Repeat until the project is fully laced. To finish lacing, take the end under the back of the last three stitches, glue in place, and trim off the excess thong. Splicing lengths of thong together is done in the same way as described earlier in the section on *Glueing* in Chapter 4. When lacing completely around a project, e.g. a handbag flap or a notecase, your thong will finish up where you began. You therefore undo the fixed end, leaving the first slit free, and an open loop of thonging with the fixed end in the second slit. With the leading end, go through the first slit, over the edge, and through the loop into the same slit as the fixed end, giving the whole of your thonging a uniform look. To set your edge lace, it should be burnished; that is, rubbed backwards and forwards with a piece of moist denim. Alternatively, you can use a wooden or plastic burnishing wheel, or a bone folder. Both of these are an inexpensive item from tool suppliers such as Tandy or Craftwares, or your local hobby shop, and they really do give your lacing a better finish.

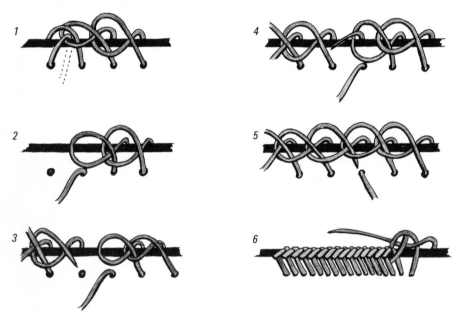

Fig. 37 Joining Spanish edge lace of two loops.

Round Edge Lacing

This is a very attractive thonging that covers the complete edge of your leather. You will need about seven or eight times the length to be thonged of lace, using about one metre or 3ft at a time and splicing where necessary. Your thonging slits should be the same distance apart as the width of your thong, and the same distance from your leather's edge, to ensure correct coverage. Working with the front towards you (following Fig. 38), take the leading end through the first slit, from the front over the edge, and through slit three (1). Then take it over, through slit five, over, through slit seven, over, through slit nine, and so on through every other slit (2) until you are one slit from the end (slit ten).

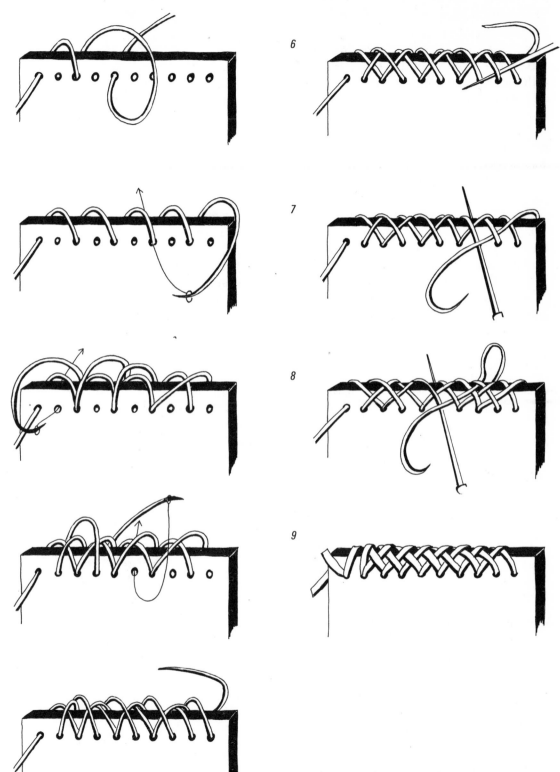

Fig. 38 Round edge lacing.

Then, with the leading end, come back over, through slits seven, five, three, and through slit two (3). Then take it over and back down your run, through the even slits (four, six, eight and ten) (4). After going through slit ten (5) and over the edge of the leather, with the help of a thonging awl to lift the thong and enlarge slits, take the leading end over the first thong to the left, under the next, and into slit eight (6). Then bring the thong over the edge of the leather, over the next thong, under the next, over and into slit six (7), over, under, over into slit four, and so on until you are back at the start (8). Here the two ends of thong should be spliced together over the edge of the leather (a), and then the thonging should be burnished.

For most of these edge lacings it is best to use continuous thonging as you can cut off the lengths you require. There are many good reels of thonging on the market, including 'Caflex', by A. Patterson & Co. Ltd., and 'English Calf Lacing' from Tandy Leather Co. I would advise $\frac{3}{32}$in (2mm) or $\frac{1}{8}$in (3mm) width thonging for most of the methods mentioned here, with the exception of Florentine lacing, for which you will need $\frac{1}{4}$in (6mm) width, in soft leather or suede lacing.

Attaching Buckles

Buckles can be attached in several ways; by stitching, thonging, press-studs or tubular rivets. The principle, though, is the same for all. Working from your belt template, make a slit for the buckle tong, allowing enough leather to wrap over and attach to the back of the belt. When you have made the slit, skive away a little of the flesh side of the leather to allow it to bend more easily.

Fig. 39 Attaching a belt or strap buckle.

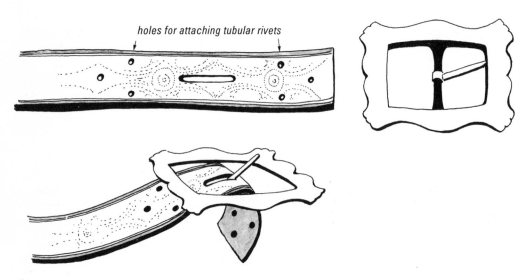

This should be done after your belt is dyed, lacquered and burnished. Attach your buckle, then wrap over the end and attach it to the belt by your chosen method. For more detail, see the photographic strip on making a belt (p. 65).

Attaching Press-studs   When attaching press-studs to projects, first check that the mark from the template is in the correct place. Then rotate your punch plier to the correct hole size (check on a piece of scrap leather first) and make your holes, one for the top and one for the bottom. Now check the four press-stud parts – two tops and two bottoms. Always make sure that you have the correct setting tools for your press-studs, which should be fitted in most cases after the project has been assembled.

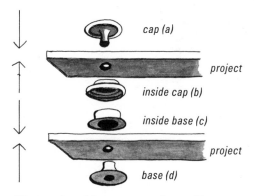

Fig. 40 Attaching a press stud: a *and* b *compress to form top,* c *and* d *compress to form bottom.*

Attaching Turn-locks   There are numerous catches for bags, but the turn-lock is by far the most popular. The position of the catch should be marked on your template, and then transferred to your leather. Turn-locks are attached when bags are fully assembled. A turn-lock has four parts; two for the bag flap, consisting of a plate with a rectangular slot cut into it and teeth on the back (a), by which it is attached to the other part – the holding plate (b). A slot of the same size should be cut into your bag flap, then the two parts pushed together, sandwiching the flap. The teeth are then bent over the holding plate with a pair of pliers, making sure that the slot in the turn-lock is in line with the slot in the leather. The other two parts consist of the actual turn-lock (c) and a holding plate (d). On the back of the turning mechanism are several small teeth, which are slotted into slits in the front of the bag, and bent over the holding plate, sandwiching the leather bag front. When the bag is closed the turn-lock should come through the slot in the flap, thus enabling the lock to be turned to fasten.

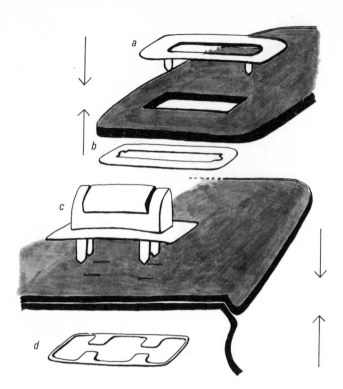

Fig. 41 Attaching a turn-lock: a and b compress to form top, c and d compress to form bottom.

Setting Eyelets

First check by experimenting with a piece of scrap leather that the punch size on the revolving plier is correct. It should be just tight around the eyelet when the hole is punched. Push the eyelet into the hole in the leather, so that the lip of the eyelet is resting on the grain side. Then, with a pair of eyelet setting pliers (easily obtainable from most haberdashery shops and hobby stores, complete with the eyelets) clasp the eyelet in the jaws of the setter and squeeze until the eyelet is set, and the edge of the eyelet on the flesh side of your leather is bevelled over.

Setting Tubular Rivets and Caps

Tubular rivets and caps come in different lengths and head sizes for different thicknesses of leather. The two parts are a (male) protruding base and a (female) inverted cap. When the correct-sized hole is made in the leather, push the base through, then place the cap on to the prong and push the two firmly together. Then lay, base down, on an anvil, and strike with a mallet, forcing them permanently together.

Burnishing and Finishing Touches

The finish is probably one of the most important parts of leather-work, hence the saying 'It's all in the finish'. An article well finished with nice clean edges and a fine shiny appearance will be

56

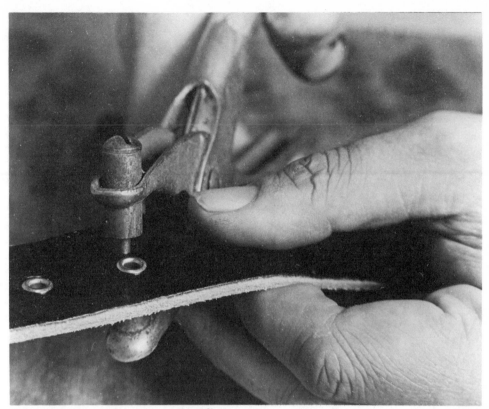

Fig. 42 Setting eyelets using setting plier.

more pleasing to the eye than a dull, raggy-edged article. If you intend to sell your work this is most important, as people's first impression of your work is what sells it. It is also a good idea to have a ticket printed with the maker's name, which can then be tied on to the bag or belt. I cannot impress upon you how much importance this final effort has in completing your project successfully, and all that is essentially required is elbow grease.

Burnishing is done on the raw edges of belts and bags, and is a method of crossing the loose fibres of the leather to form a hard edge. First, on seamed edges of bags, etc. you should shave off any excess leather with a sharp knife, or saddler's spoke shave, until the edges of the attached pieces are level and smooth. Then, with an edge-beveller, run round the edges of the seams, taking off the sharp corners. You should now have a nicely rounded and level exposed edge. You will need to dye this in, using a water dye. For burnishing I would recommend a product called 'Dyamine'. Edges are usually dyed in black, either with a small felt dauber, or a felt pen filled with dye. Then, when the edges are covered, rub over vigorously with a piece of denim or hessian. This should give you a fine burnished edge. Alternatively, you can rub over with a bone folder or a burnishing wheel, but basically to burnish well

Fig. 43 Setting tubular rivets and caps.

requires plenty of vigorous rubbing back and forth, no matter what is used.

When burnishing belts, pull the belt through a damp denim cloth, so that both edges are in contact with the cloth. Repeat this several times, then do it with a piece of dry denim. Again, repeat several times, until the edge is well smoothed, and there are no loose fibres. There are several edge finishes available, including those by Fiebing, Tandy and Omega. If you are edging a belt where the edges are not dyed, apply a black or brown water dye with a felt dauber, then burnish as above.

When all the edges of your project are burnished, you are ready to polish it. Use an oil, cream or liquid for polishing; analine cream is good, so is saddle soap. It is up to you to choose whichever in your opinion gives you the best shine. I use a 'Meltonian Analine Cream Polish', in the same colour as I have dyed my work. This, when applied on a small sponge and polished off with a soft brush or cloth, gives a good rich shine. When you have done all this, and your project is complete, sit back and admire your handiwork.

The following two photostrips show how I set about making a bag and a belt and they will serve to recap on what you have learnt so far.

Photostrip: Making a Single-compartment Bag

1

First, having made sure that my pattern template is absolutely correct in all its measurements, I mark out around each template on to the grain side of the leather. All the various parts of the bag should run the same way across the leather, so that the grain on the finished bag runs from top to bottom rather than from side to side.

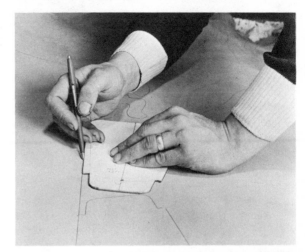

2

When all the parts of the bag are marked, I start to cut them out, cutting the straight edges first (along a steel ruler) and then cutting the various curves and corners on each piece. It is much easier to cut a corner on this side, for instance, once it is freed from the main bulk of the leather.

3

With all the pieces cut out I can now mark my crease lines, using a screw crease. Where I intend to stitch, I mark only a single line on the leather, about ¼in (6mm) from the edge. On pieces that are not stitched, such as the bag flap and the tongue of this catch, a second crease line about ⅛in (3mm) from the first looks most attractive. This is easily achieved by opening my screw crease ⅛in (3mm) wider, and pulling around the edge of the leather.

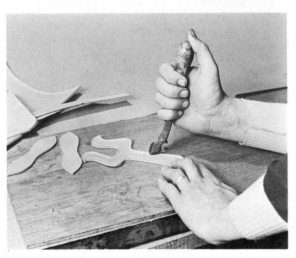

4

All my bag parts are now creased, so I am bevelling some of the edges with a number 3 edge shave. I am bevelling only the parts which will not be stitched, where I have double crease lines – like the flap, catch tongue, strap, and the tops of the sides. I bevel all these on both the grain and flesh sides. When this is done I am ready to dye my bag.

5

With plenty of newspaper on my dye bench, and my tools well clear, I apply a generous coat of dark brown dye, using a sheepskin pad and rubbing in a circular movement until the surface is covered. Allowing a little time in between, I apply two or three coats until the leather has a good rich brown colour. I have also given the back flesh side one coat of dye. Now I can allow it to dry thoroughly for about half an hour.

6

My bag is now dry, and I have brushed over all the parts in order to remove any dye residue (a fine powder sometimes left on the leather). I am now applying a thin coat of leather lacquer, using a pad made from a square of material wrapped around some cotton wool.

Using circular strokes I apply lacquer to all my bag parts, leaving a fine sheen on them.

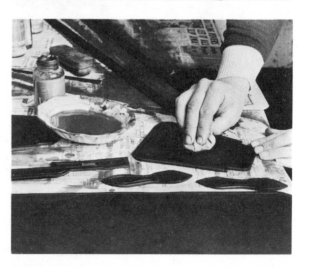

7

I am now ready to start stitch-marking all the various pieces. In this instance the main body of the bag is to be stitched to the sides, so I need only mark this part, and not the sides, as when all the parts have been glued together one series of stitch-marks on the front will be sufficient to follow. On this bag I am using about eight stitches to the inch (or 25mm)

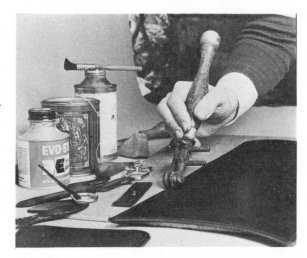

8

Dee rings needed to hold the shoulder strap are glued into the holder, and firmly pressed together. I have to attach these to the side of the bag.

9

Setting the dee ring in place on the centre of the side, I can now mark around it, and then rough up the leather surface on both the back of the dee ring holder and the side of the bag (inside my mark), thus making a suitable surface for the glue to hold the dee ring in place for stitching.

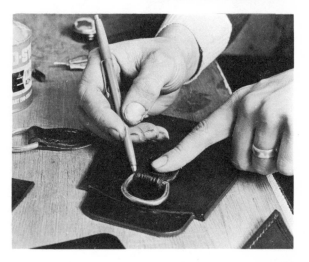

10

Sometimes, where a thick piece of leather such as this buckle holder is to be attached, it is necessary to shave or skive off a little of the leather in order to reduce the thickness. Both this surface and the surface to which it will be attached will also need roughening.

11

Here I am glueing the buckle in place on the front of the bag. I have spread contact adhesive on both roughened surfaces and allowed it to dry to the touch. I can now push them together, firmly in place.

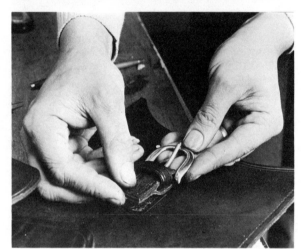

12

Using a saddle stitch I now sew on the buckle, and all the other small parts such as the catch tongue and dee ring holders, as these can all be very difficult to attach after the main body of the bag is assembled.

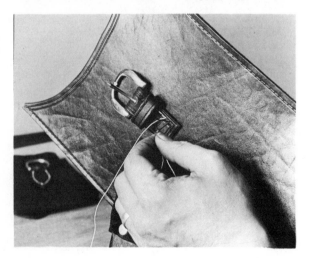

13

Having attached the buckle, tongue and dee ring holders, I can now glue the first side of the bag in place ready for stitching, making sure that the edges are as level with each other as possible.

14

Using a saddle stitch, I now stitch the side in place. Notice that the needle is in the crossed swords position, as described in the section on Stitching *on p. 44. Having stitched the first side in place, I will repeat the same process – glueing and stitching the other side in place. My bag will then be fully assembled.*

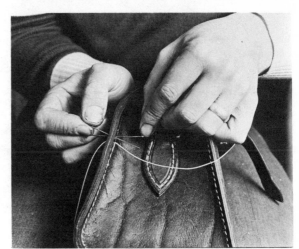

15

I am now levelling up the edges, using a spokeshave to shave off any overhanging leather and make both sides even. This can also be done with a sharp knife. Great care must be taken to get the two edges of the leather just level, without shaving off too close to your stitched seam.
The spokeshave I am using is an ordinary wooden one, with the blade sharpened a little. After I have shaved the edge, I will rub it over with a piece of medium sandpaper, to give it a smooth, level edge.

16

This edge will now be bevelled on both sides to round it up, again using a number 3 edge shave. You will now see why I did not edge bevel the edges in step 4, for if I had they would have been shaved off. This is why, on seamed edges, I leave it until this stage. After bevelling the edges of my bag I will dye the raw colour in with some edge dye, and burnish them with a piece of denim and a bone folder until they have a smooth edge, and the side and body pieces of the bag look as one piece of leather, with no visible join on the seam.

17

With all the edges now burnished, the strap may now be attached. Here I am doing it with two small tubular rivets, but the shoulder strap could equally well be stitched on, or a press-stud used should you want a detachable strap.

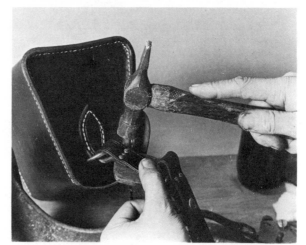

18

This is the completed bag, which has been polished up with a dark brown analine cream.

Photostrip: Making a Belt

1

Making sure my hide is long enough for the length of belt I require, I cut a straight line down the edge of my leather along a steel ruler. The cut should be straight and even, using enough pressure for the knife to cut in one stroke, and leaving a clean and level edge.

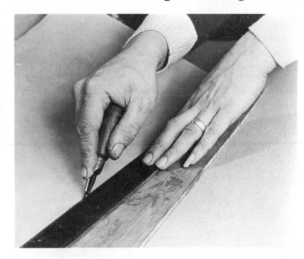

2

Having selected a buckle, I measure the inside opening required for the width of the belt.

3

I now set my plough knife to the same measurement, and cut my strip by pushing the knife up through the leather with an even stroke, keeping the edge of the leather hard against the guard of the plough knife. In this way I get a uniform width all the way through my strip of leather.

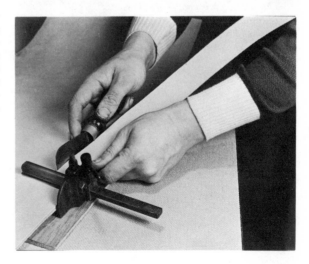

4

Once the strip of leather is cut, I can now mark one end of the belt from my template. Then I measure the belt's length with a tape measure, and mark the other end from the template. Then I can cut off the ends.

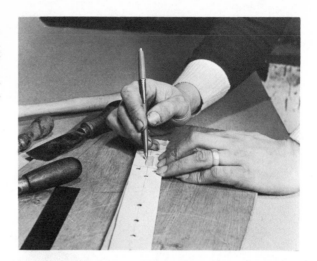

5

The two ends of the belt are now cut out, and I can make a crease line down the belt about ¼in (6mm) from the edge. I then repeat this, making another line about an ⅛in (3mm) from the first, which gives me a deep double crease line.

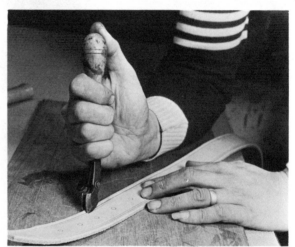

6

The belt length is now ready to be edge-bevelled, using a number 3 edge shave and bevelling both grain and flesh sides of the belt.

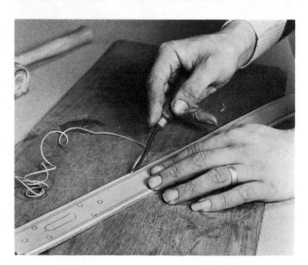

7

Now I take out the slit for the buckle tongue with a crew punch.

8

I now punch a series of fitting holes with my six-way plier. The tube size used should be large enough to fit the buckle tongue.

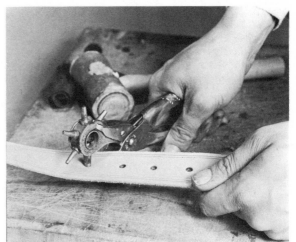

9

The belt is now ready to be dyed. I find the best way with such items as belts and straps is to dip-dye them. This is done by running the belt through a tray of dye, so that both flesh and grain sides of the leather are dyed in one operation. I then place the belt on some newspaper, and wipe off any excess dye with a sponge. After allowing the belt to dry for about half an hour, I treat it with a leather lacquer or finish.

10

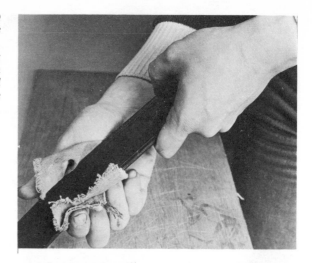

When the belt is dry, I burnish the edges to give them a smooth finish. The best way to do this with belts and straps is to pull the belt through a piece of denim or hessian several times, until all the loose fibres are smoothed into the edge.

11

Where the belt is to be bent over the buckle bar, it needs to be thinner in order to allow it to bend more easily. I do this by skiving away a little of the thickness of the leather.

12

Once the buckle end of the belt is sufficiently thinned, I can attach the buckle. Here, I am attaching the buckle with tubular rivets and caps, but press-studs can also be used, thus allowing the buckle to be interchanged with others of the same width. For a more expensive finish, the buckle could be stitched or thonged in place.

13
To complete the belt you need a
keeper. This is a loop of leather used
to keep the end of the belt in place,
and is made from a piece of leather
about ¾in (18mm) in width, and
long enough to go round the belt, the
ends being joined either by riveting
or sewing.

14
A good polish, and you have a
completed belt.

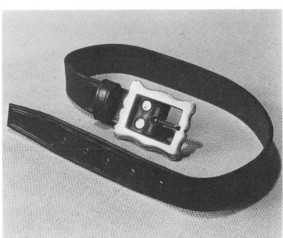

Decorative Techniques 5

It is in this section of the book that I intend to talk about the various ways of decorating your work. In the previous chapters we have discussed making plain projects, but after you have completed and are proficient at plain projects you will want to try decorating them perhaps by means of carving, embossing, modelling or moulding. It is up to you to decide which kind of decoration to put on a project; sometimes you will find that a plain, sophisticated look to, say, a bag, is far more suitable than covering it with masses of decoration. Leather, being such a versatile material, has endless possibilities for decoration. It is a soft, yet strong, material upon which impressions can easily be made, as you will have seen with creasing. It can also be stretched, bent, and sewn together to build into the most intricate projects.

Embossing

This is the technique of building patterns by making impressions with various objects. There are many tools which can be bought from some of the American, English and German tool companies; most good hobby shops also stock them. They include all sorts of designs such as horse shoes, stars, bucking broncos, and many others. One can also use carving tools, as you will see later. For the mass-produced market there are also stamps called 'Boss Buttons', with embossing designs on them. These are used in a small machine called a Clicker Press, which will force the impression into the leather with a pressure of one ton. There are also embossing wheels, and machines that will emboss a belt length in a matter of seconds, and although the designs are numerous, they take a little skill and imagination to use. I feel that it is far more

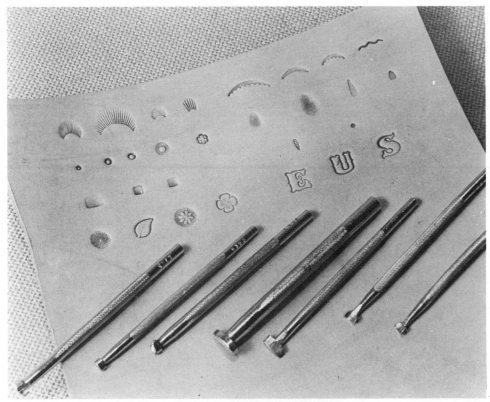

Fig. 44 Embossing and carving tools and impressions made.

interesting and exciting to build up your own patterns with small abstract tools, working up to a mandella type pattern.

Tools can be bought, but can also be made from screws, nails and bolts by filing and sawing into the ends with a small hacksaw; in this way interesting and imaginative patterns can be made. To do this, start by sawing off the point of, say, a 6in (15cm) nail, thus making it flat. Then turn it upside down, and cut or file pattern into the flat head of the nail. Then, by banging the head of the nail into the lightly moistened leather, a fine impression can be made. Impressions can also be made with an infinite number of items such as forks, bottle openers, and even coins, so you see there is no real need to go to the expense of buying ready-made embossing tools for the job. These are only time savers in a lot of cases; it doesn't take a great craftsman to emboss a four-leaf clover design into a piece of leather using a ready-made stamp. It does, however, show some skill and imagination to build an interesting pattern using tools made from nails, bolts and screws. The one concession I will make to ready-made stamps, however, is in the case of some of the sets of Alphabet stamps. These can be very useful for monogrammed articles, and are very difficult to make oneself.

Fig. 45 Example of embossing and tools used. As you see, quite an interesting pattern may be made using these few tools.

When you have made an embossed pattern on your project, whether it is a bag flap, hat brim, or belt, you can either dye it in one colour, or, by using the technique explained in the section on *Dyeing Embossing* in Chapter 3, multi-colour dye it. This gives a very attractive finish.

For embossing, you will need a piece of smooth marble, or a slate slab, of substantial thickness. You will also need a rawhide mallet, and some embossing tools. Embossing is always done before the project is dyed or made up. For example, if you are embossing a bag flap, cut out all the bag parts, crease and edge them, and then carry out your embossing by placing the bag flap flesh side down on the marble slab. Lightly moisten the leather with cold water, then position the embossing tool in the required place and holding it vertical, strike firmly with the mallet. Remove the tool, and you should have a clear impression left on the leather.

Fig. 46 Using a basket-weave tool. (Note guideline.)

Repeat until your pattern is completely built up, and when you are satisfied wash the leather down with some cleaner (see Chapter 1, *Cleaners*) to remove any marks you may have made while working on the pattern. You are then ready to dye and assemble your work. Needless to say, practise embossing on scrap leather until you are happy with your patterns.

Embossing, and similarly carving, should only be done on vegetable or oak bark tanned leather of a substance not under 2mm ($\frac{3}{32}$in) thick, as if you try to emboss fine leathers you are likely to go right through them.

Some embossing tools will make a basket weave pattern, which is fairly fast to do, and which looks very effective on belts, straps, etc., as it creates the effect of the leather actually having been woven. This should also be practised on a piece of scrap leather first. For a basket weave you need to mark a guide line down the centre of your belt or strap, then starting from the centre, make your first stamp above the line, then your second stamp below the line, so that the top of the second stamp is joined to the bottom of the first stamp. The third stamp should then be made above the line, so that the bottom of it joins the top of the second stamp, and so on, until the basket weave is built up. This can also be done diagonally, or even used as a random stamp.

Embossing is a fairly simple, but most effective, way of using your imagination to enhance your projects.

Leather Carving

Leather carving is one of the most impressive and intricate-looking ways of decorating leather. Its origins lie back in the days when the Spanish Conquistadores introduced their highly decorative leatherwork to the Indians of South America. At that time their work consisted mainly of geometric designs, but they were so intrigued with the plant life found in the New World that they began to stylise and transfer the plant and flower designs to leather. Carving, or tooling as it is sometimes known, spread rapidly from Mexico across USA, and now seems to be getting more and more popular throughout the world. When I first started to carve leather all the tools had to be ordered and sent from USA, but now, because of its growing popularity, carving tools are freely available world-wide.

Carving is a process of forming intricate patterns on the leather by a series of cuts or incisions. None of the leather is actually cut away, but the effect achieved by backgrounding and shading the leather, and then lifting the foreground into high relief with small saddle stamp tools, gives the impression that the leather has been cut away. It takes a lot of practice and a very steady hand to become proficient at carving.

Carving Patterns

There are many sources of carving patterns. They can be found in bought pattern books, from which you trace the pattern and then transfer it to your leather by going over the tracing with a ballpoint pen or pointed modeller until the pattern is impressed on the leather. You can also buy ready-made plastic templates which when placed on the leather, and rubbed across the back with a spoon modeller, leave the pattern's impression. Patterns can also be obtained from many things, such as brass rubbings, drawings, ornate wood carvings on furniture, ornate brass door knockers – in fact there are all kinds of places in which you will find designs suitable for transferring to leather. You will therefore find it useful to always carry some tracing paper on you, so that you can take tracings of designs you see, and gradually build up a collection of suitable and original designs for leather carving.

74

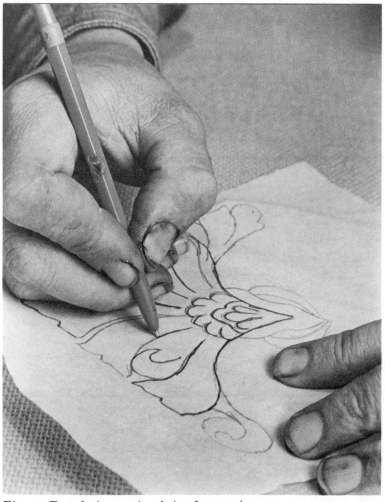

Fig. 47 Transferring carving design from tracing.

Transferring the Pattern on to the Leather

The correct leather for tooling is a cowhide of not under 2mm ($\frac{3}{32}$in) thick. It should be unglazed, and either vegetable or oak bark tanned, and before the design is transferred it should be fully cased by submersion in cold water for a few minutes. It should then be laid flat until the colour of the grain returns to how it was when dry. Your design should be traced on to tracing paper with a pencil, following the lines carefully, and when it is complete, placed on the cased leather. It can be kept in place with some tape or paper clips while you go over the design, pressing lightly with an old ballpoint pen or a pointed modeller, until you have retraced all the lines. You must make sure that all the lines are retraced, otherwise you will be left with gaps in your design. If you are using a ready-made template, place it with the raised side down on your cased leather, then with a modelling spoon or even the back of an old teaspoon rub firmly over the back of the template until an impression is made.

The *swivel knife* is definitely one of the most important tools in leather carving. With it you actually cut out the design, allowing the pattern to be brought into relief with the stamping tools. A swivel knife is also used on the completed carving to make decorative cuts, which will greatly enhance one's carving. The way to use a swivel knife is to hold it with your forefinger on the yoke at the top of the knife, and with your thumb and middle finger hold the barrel of the knife. Then, by turning your thumb and middle finger you can turn the blade the correct way to cut. The cutting is done by dragging the blade towards you, using your thumb and middle finger to steer it, whilst applying the pressure with your forefinger to determine the depth of the cut. Always keep the blade upright, so that you achieve a straight cut. In this way, cut all the lines in your tracing, being careful not to cut through other lines, and not to overshoot on the ends of lines. When all the traced lines of the pattern are cut, you will be ready to begin your stamping.

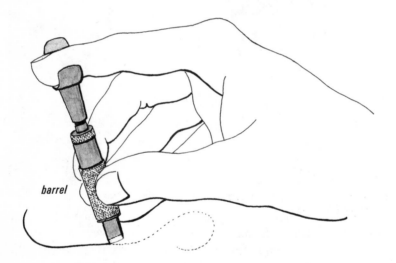

barrel

Fig. 48 Correct way of holding swivel knife. Cut should be made by pulling the knife towards you.

A *camouflage tool* is used for patterning parts of your design. It is used by placing it on the leather, and striking it with a rawhide mallet, which creates an impression on the surface of the leather. The impressions can be altered by varying the position of the tool, rocking it on its sides or back. It can be used in an infinite variety of ways to create all kinds of effects. *Veiner tools* are used in the same way as camouflage tools, and again are used to enhance certain parts of your design. They are called veiner tools because as their name suggests, they are especially used for creating veins

Fig. 49 Cutting round the traced lines of your carving pattern.

on the leaves of designs, although they also have a wide variety of other uses for creating pattern effects. *Seeder tools* are used for putting seeds in the centres of flowers, and so on. *Pear shaders* are used to bruise the edges of flower petals, leaves, etc. With this tool you can create a really stunning effect. It is used by striking with a mallet while walking the head of the tool around the area to be shaded, using the thumb and forefinger. Pear shaders have a variety of finishes; chequered, ribbed, lined and plain. It is up to you to pick the finish which is most suited to your carving. Always make sure that the surface of the leather is well cased (moistened) before using pear shading tools, in order to obtain the best effect. The *beveller* is the tool which actually brings your carving into relief. It is used by placing the toe on to the cut left by your swivel knife, then striking the top of the tool with a mallet, thus depressing one side of the cut and raising the side against which the toe rested. By varying the force of the blow with the mallet you can create different depths to the design. Again, for the best effect this tool should be walked along the line; this is done by moving the tool along slightly after each blow with the mallet, until you build up a rhythm, leaving an evenly bevelled edge. In this way you

Fig. 50 Using camouflage tool. (Note correct way of holding tool.)

bevel around the entire pattern until it is built into complete relief, leaving some areas raised and others depressed. Bevelling should never appear jerky; if it does, this means that either the beveller is not being held straight, or it is not being walked along uniformly. Both of these faults can be corrected with a little practice. After bevelling, you can go around the edges of the bevelled line with a modelling spoon, just to smooth them in.

Once your complete design is bevelled, a *background tool* is used to depress the background areas and make the design stand out in stronger relief. A good background tool is one which is pointed at one end for tight areas, and is wider at the other end for larger areas. This tool is held straight up and struck with uniform blows to create an evenly stippled background effect. Be careful though – if you strike too hard, you are in danger of going right through the leather.

Fig. 51 Using veiner tool, and effect created.

Decorative Cuts   Once your design is complete, you can go over it lightly in certain places with your swivel knife, to enhance the carving. Swivel cuts need to be practised before risking your finished carving. They are usually applied to flower petals, leaves, and stems. Once this is done, your carving is complete, and ready for dyeing.

Carving is a fascinating and effective way of decorating leather, and the more you practise the better you will become. It does take time to master the technique properly, so if this is what you want to do keep working at it.

There are many, many different stamps available, but by no means do you need them all. It is up to you to decide which ones you will need to suit the designs you intend to carve.

I have only covered the elementaries of leather carving here; if you wish to go further in this branch of leatherwork I suggest you

Fig. 52 Embossing seeds with seeder tool.

look at some of the more specialised books devoted entirely to carving, some of which are listed in the bibliography at the end of this book. Above all, remember – enjoy your leatherwork. If it pleases you, it should please others.

Decorative Stitching

This is when you use stitching for patterning your work rather than holding it together, although the two reasons can sometimes be combined. Saddle stitching can be used, or a simple running stitch as it will not be taking any strain. You can use any of millions of designs for transferring on to leather – embroidery patterns of flowers, animals, geometric patterns, and so on.

It is best to dye your work first; then, before assembling it, transfer the outline of your design on to the leather by making a

Fig. 53 Using pear shader. (Note bruised effect on leaves.)

faint impression through some tracing paper with an old ballpoint pen or pointed modelling tool. Once the impression has been made, go over the lines with a stitch-marker. Then, with your awl, pierce all the holes. You then stitch around them, thus creating your design. Always remember to cast off at the back of your work, to keep it looking tidy. Some effect can be created by stitching in contrasting colours, such as yellow thread on black leather, or beige on dark brown leather. You can even combine different colour cottons – green for leaves, red for flowers, and so on.

Use your imagination to create exciting and interesting patterns with needle and thread; you will be surprised at the effects you can achieve. The key to good decorative stitching is to keep all your stitches neat, evenly spaced, and going the same way.

Fig. 54 Bevelling the design. This tool should be walked along backwards and forwards until design is raised to the height you require.

Appliqué Work

Appliqué work is a form of laminating a leather design on to a project. It is normally stitched on, but it can also be studded on, using tubular rivets. The design can be as ornate as you like, although very sharp points tend to be more difficult to attach, and curl up with wear.

You can use a variety of materials for appliqué: suede, soft leather, snakeskin, in either matching or constrasting colours. The design may be of flat leather, which is sewn on to the project, or a more complex raised design lifted from underneath.

For a flat design it is best to start by making a template, then cut your leather or suede from that. When the project is dyed and ready for assembly, mark round your appliqué template on to the project. Once this is done, lightly score the surface within the outline so that you attain better adhesion when you glue the appliqué in place. When you have glued the appliqué, stitch-mark

Fig. 55 Background tool.

it and then neatly sew it in place. If you wish to make several layers of appliqué, stitch them together before you glue and stitch them to your project.

For a raised appliqué, you will also need a pattern template from which your pattern should be cut. You will then need to cut another pattern about ½in (12mm) smaller all round, and from a thicker piece of leather. Then, from your template, mark, score and glue the area on your project where the appliqué is to go. With the edge shave, bevel one edge of the thicker, smaller piece of leather and glue this into the middle of the area on your project, allowing ½in (12mm) of space all round. Once this is dry, glue the top of it, plus the underpart of the appliqué. If the appliqué is a thick leather, it may be necessary to skive it down around the edge before glueing it into place. Once it is in place, smooth all the edges down and begin stitching, using the saddle stitch. This will

Fig. 56 Completed design with decorative cuts; is now ready for dyeing.

pull down the edge of the appliqué, leaving a nice raised effect where it is stretched over the thicker piece of leather which has been sandwiched in the middle.

The possibilities with appliqués are endless – they can be patterned, plain, contrasting colours, contrasting stitching; they can have decorative studs in them, or they can be thonged, sewn, or studded to your projects. Appliqué can be used to decorate bag flaps, belts, or in fact almost any project, and for the effect obtained it is relatively simple to do.

Decorating with Rivets and Studs

There is a very wide variety of studs available, of all shapes and sizes; stars, crescents, horse shoes, diamonds, clover leaves; studs inset with glass jewels, flat-headed studs, pyramid and oval studs. It is a simple matter to build up patterns on your work with these,

Fig. 57 Example of decorative stitching.

most of which have wire prongs on the back, and are attached by pushing the prongs through the leather, then bending them over on the back to secure. Decorative studs are easily obtainable from hobby shops or leather sundry suppliers. Other brass and metal items, such as horse brasses, eyelet washers and so on, can also be used with effect for decorating leather. When you are conversant with leatherwork you will find yourself viewing everything with an eye to utilising it to enhance your work.

Modelling This is a technique similar to embossing, but whereas embossing is done on the grain side of the leather, modelling is done from the flesh side to make the pattern stand out in relief. First, transfer the design lightly on to the grain side of your leather. Then, with a pointed modeller, go round the lines of the design until a deep

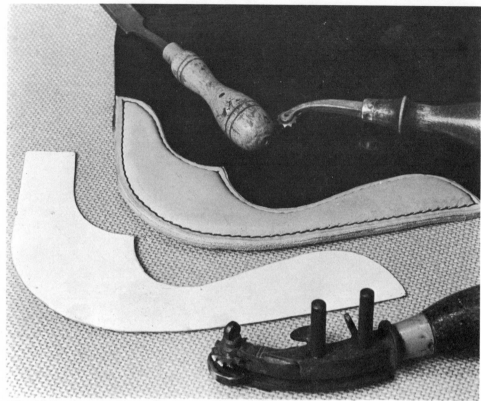

Fig. 58 Completed raised appliqué showing cardboard template.

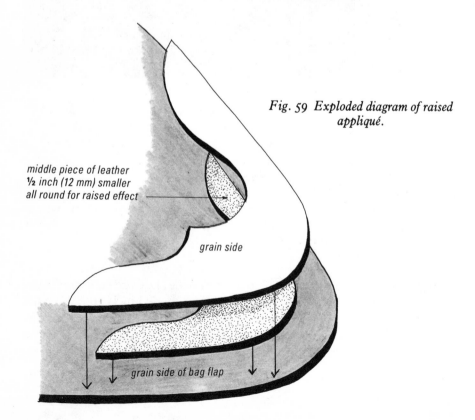

Fig. 59 Exploded diagram of raised appliqué.

middle piece of leather
½ inch (12 mm) smaller
all round for raised effect

grain side

grain side of bag flap

Fig. 60 Some examples of the numerous rivets and studs available with which to decorate your work.

impression is made, so that when the leather is turned over you can see the impression on the flesh side. Now hold the work in one hand, and with a spoon or ball-end modelling tool in the other, begin to raise your design by rubbing to and fro on the flesh side, within the outlines of your pattern. This will push up your design on the grain side of the leather. When you have achieved an even raising of the pattern, lay the leather flesh side down on a flat piece of stone or marble, and trace round the outside of the pattern with a pointed modeller, to re-define the outline. The hollows which are left can now be filled in with liquid cork or papier mâché in order to make them more permanent. Modelling should really only be done on projects that are to be lined, or book covers, where the back is hidden, so that the filler does not show. It can make a very attractive decoration for your work, and numerous patterns can be used, as long as they are fairly open patterns which allow plenty of room for the raising.

Moulding   This is for making such things as leather mugs and bottles, sword scabbards, and so on. It is a method of wet-moulding the leather

87

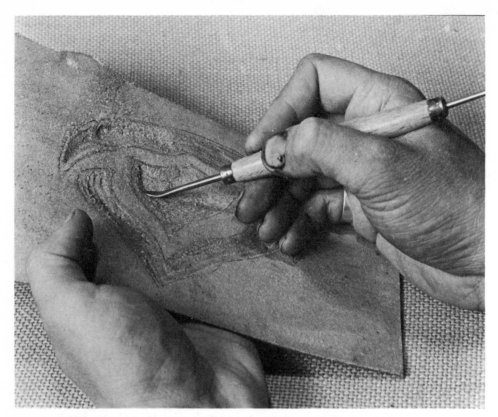

Fig. 61 *Raising the design from the flesh side using a modelling tool.*

over a former (wooden block) and then stretching it to shape. The technique dates back to before the Middle Ages, when it was used for making Black Jacks and leather bottles. An example of moulding is where you want to make a purse without sewing in side gussets. First, make your purse flat, by sewing the front piece of leather to the back piece. Then cut a wooden block ½in (12mm)

Fig. 62 *Forcing wooden block into purse to achieve stretch.*

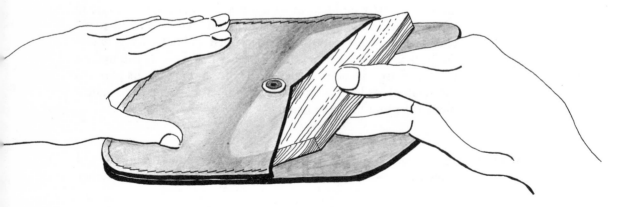

Fig. 63 Completed modelling showing tracing pattern and modelling tools.

smaller than the inside of the purse, and about 1in (25mm) thick. Now soak your flat purse in warm water, until it becomes soft and supple, and then force the wooden block into the purse, stretching the leather. Allow it to dry thoroughly before removing the block. You should then be left with a nice wide purse. This is one simple use of moulding, but as leather is a material which becomes extremely soft and pliable when wet, it can be moulded to any shape, to make purses, hats, bags, holsters, knife sheaths, and so on. If you should want to harden the leather, to make, say, a waste paper bin, this can be done by wetting in the same way, and then force-drying in the sun or in front of a warm oven. You must, however, be careful not to apply too much heat, as this will shrivel the leather.

Weaving and Plaiting

To make attractive belts and wrist-bands, or handbag straps, leather can be plaited and woven together. Any girl who has plaited her hair can show you how to do a simple plait. There are also trick plaits, so-called because the plait has no joins in it. The simplest is the three-thong plait, which is ideal for making wrist-

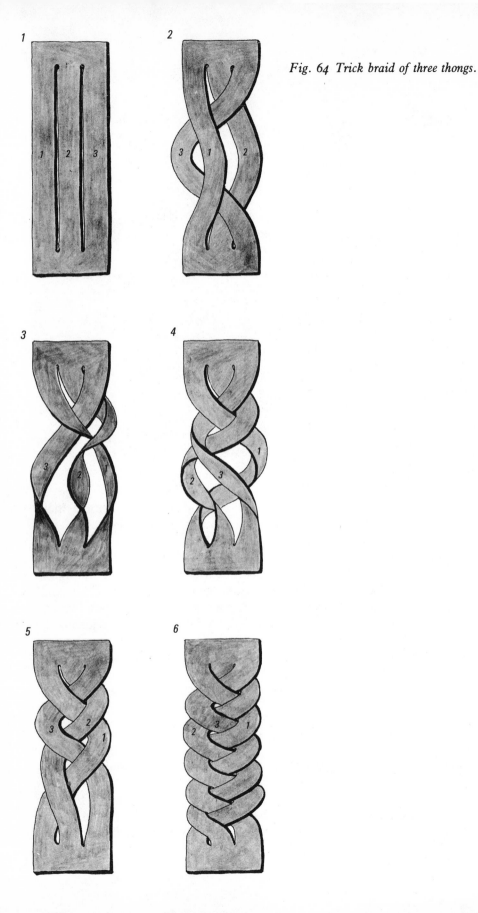

Fig. 64 *Trick braid of three thongs.*

bands, belts and straps. You must first determine the length of the leather strip; if you are making a belt, allow about a quarter of the total length again, for shrinkage, when the leather is plaited. If the width of the belt is to be 1½in (36mm), cut three equal strips of ½in (12mm), leaving both ends uncut. Now punch a small hole at the end of each slit, in order to stop the leather from tearing. Lightly case the leather, then begin the plaiting in the following way. First take thong three over thong two, and under thong one. This will twist the bottom of the plait and so to straighten it take the entire bottom through the middle of thongs one and two. Thong two is then placed over thong one, and thong three over thong two. The entire bottom is then taken through the gap between thongs one and two. Carry on in this way until the entire length is plaited. The plait should appear tight at the top and loose at the bottom; it can then be evened out by loosening, working from the bottom up. This trick plait can also be done with five or seven strands.

Slit plaiting is another simple method of making a plait by using a piece of strap doubled over, and then making vertical slits in both pieces of leather. You then pass the alternate straps back and forth through the slits.

Fig. 65 *Slit plaiting. Ideal way of attaching belt or strap buckle.*

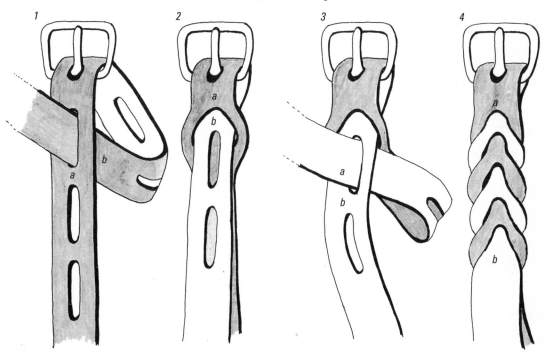

This was sold a few years ago as 'Scoobie doo', for children to make. It is an attractive braid with which to make key fobs, dog leads, and handles for bags and cases. Once you get the hang of it, it is an easy thing to do in your leisure time whilst watching television and so on. I have often sat in my shop doing this braid, and it is ideal for long train journeys.

You start with two pieces of lace of equal length, which you interlace as in diagram 1 (Fig. 66). Pull the ends tight, as in diagram 2, then fold thongs 2 and 2a over in opposite directions. Take thong 1 over thong 2 and under thong 2a, then take thong 1a over thong 2a and under thong 2, as in diagram 3. Your work should then appear as in diagram 4. By tightening the thong you should arrive at a neat square, as in diagram 5. Now you are ready to do the next braid, which is done in exactly the same way, only from the right-hand side, as in diagram 6. Tighten as shown in diagram 7, and continue until your braided length has been achieved. This should appear as in diagram 8. To finish off your braid, the last thong can either be glued in place, or the cut-off ends can be tucked back in under the last bend, as in diagram 8.

Fig. 66 Four-thong square braid.

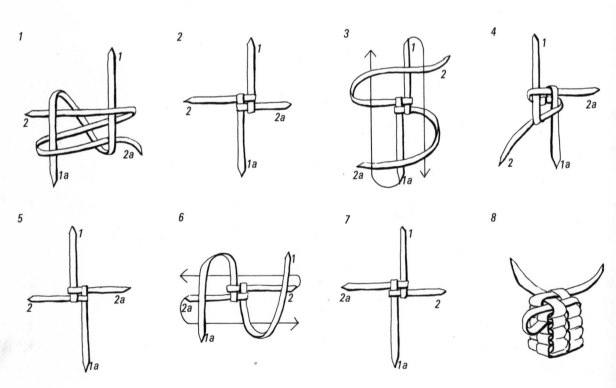

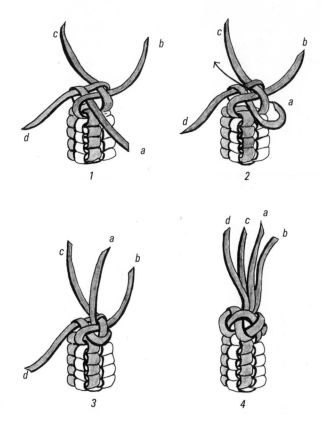

Fig. 67 Turk's Head knot.

*Finishing Off a
Four-thong Braid with
a Turk's Head Knot*

For such things as dog leads, turk's head knots are an attractive way of finishing off a four-thong braid (Fig. 67). You should finish with the flesh side up as in diagram 1, then take thong a round the outside and under thongs b and c, emerging through the centre, as in diagram 2. Then take thong d around and up through thongs c and d, again emerging in the centre as in diagram 3. Then take thong b under and up in the same manner, and finally thong c, ending up by pulling all the thongs tight to form the knot, as in diagram 4.

*Criss-cross Thong
Appliqué*

This is an attractive form of decoration for belts, bags, purses, and so on (see Fig. 68). To make it most effective, the distance between the holes and the space between the two vertical rows should be judged according to the width of the thong used, i.e. if you are using ⅛in (3mm) thong, the holes should be spaced about ⅛in (3mm) apart, and the rows should be about 1in (2·5cm) apart. Pass the leading end of the thong through the first hole on the right-hand side, from the back, into the second hole on the left-hand side, and out of the first hole on the left, as in diagram 1. Then take the leading end through the third hole on the right, out of the second hole on the right, as in diagram 2, then through the third hole on the left and out of the second hole on the left, as in diagram 3. Then take it through holes four and three on the right, and holes four and three on the left, as in diagram 5, then holes five and four on the right, as in diagram 6. Continue until the woven length is complete, as shown in diagram 7, then secure the ends on the back, as illustrated in diagram 8.

Fig. 68 Criss-cross appliqué.

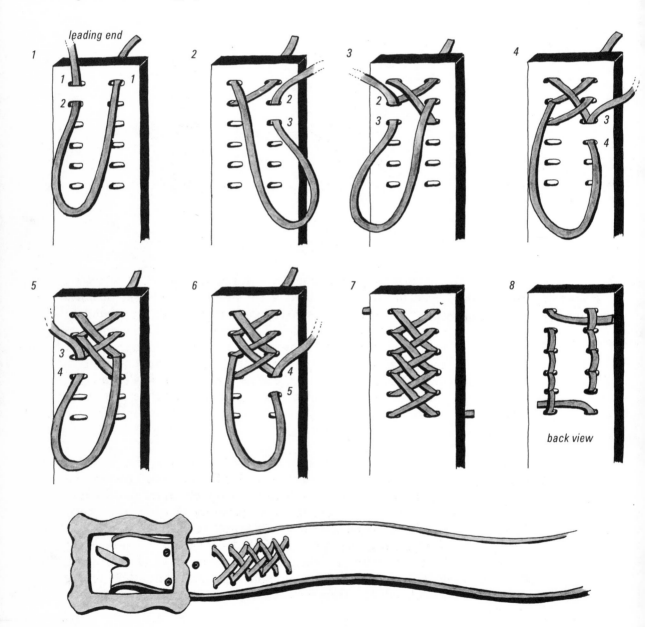

Projects

Fig. 69 A good display of attractive and practical projects. Instructions for these are on the following pages.

In this section of the book I have included patterns for eleven items, ranging from simple projects such as hair slides and key rings, to more complicated items such as handbags and purses. As to the decoration of these items, some I have left plain, and for others I have given examples of patterning ideas. These are only illustrated in the photographs of the completed items, and I have purposely not included any decorations on the patterns for the various projects, as I think it is important for you to use your own imagination for these ideas.

The patterns and instructions included are, when used to their best advantage, a way of making you familiar with the design and construction of these items. It is important that as you become proficient at leathercraft you make variations on these designs, eventually progressing to designs of your own. An example of this is the small pleated neck-purse shown in Project 6; this could also be used as a belt-purse, or handbag pocket, and with only a slight variation to the pattern it could also be enlarged to make a single-compartment handbag. So you see, there is an infinite variety of uses to which these basic patterns can be put.

I cannot emphasise enough how important it is to use your own imagination to brand your personality on to your work. By all means start by making these projects as they are, but after a while vary them, and use patterns of your own – even if at first they are only modifications of these patterns – otherwise you might as well go out and buy a leatherwork kit.

I hope that by making these projects you will achieve a good deal of satisfaction, as I did when designing them for this book.

Note: the following projects are marked in imperial measurements, but they have been drawn on metric graph paper. This means that you can make up the projects according to which system of measurement you prefer – by following either the written measurements or the graph lines.

Project 1 – Hairslides

You will need:

some pieces of scrap leather, 3mm ($\frac{1}{8}$in)
small quantity of dye
knife
ruler
screw crease
$\frac{3}{16}$in (4·5mm) round punch
number 3 edge shave
small length of dowelling, $\frac{3}{16}$in (4·5mm) in diameter
pencil sharpener
small sheet of stiff card

Firstly, trace the pattern on to your card for either slide a or slide b. Then, cut out the card template, including the two holes. Place this on the leather and draw round. Now cut out, using your knife and ruler. Punch the two holes out, using the $\frac{3}{16}$in (4·5mm) punch. Take the screw crease, open to about $\frac{3}{16}$in (4·5mm), and crease a line all around, repeating if two lines are required. Now, with the number 3 edge shave, bevel all the edges on both sides. Next, cut off a 5in (12·5cm) length of dowel, and sharpen one end to a point with the pencil sharpener. The slide is now ready for dyeing, unless you wish to pattern it by embossing or carving, which needs to be done before the dyeing. Decorative work such as appliqué, decorative stitching or decorative stud work, can all be done when the slide has been dyed. Once both the slide and the dowel have been dyed and polished, insert the dowel into the holes, and the slide is complete.

Project 2 – Keyrings

You will need:

some small scrap pieces of 3mm ($\frac{1}{8}$in) leather
1in (25mm) split ring
tubular rivets and caps
knife
number 3 edge shave
screw crease
six-way punch plier
dye
cardboard

Trace the pattern for either keyring a, b, or c on to the cardboard, and cut out. Place your cardboard template on to the leather, draw round, and cut out. Set the screw crease at about $\frac{3}{16}$in (4·5mm), and put a crease line all the way round. Bevel front and back edges with the number 3 edge shave. Apply any embossing or carving required, then dye and polish. Insert the split ring, and attach the rivet as shown in diagram A. The keyring is then complete. Any additional patterning such as decorative stitching or studs, should be applied after the keyring has been dyed, but before the split ring is attached.

Project 1 – Hairslides
Project 2 – Keyrings

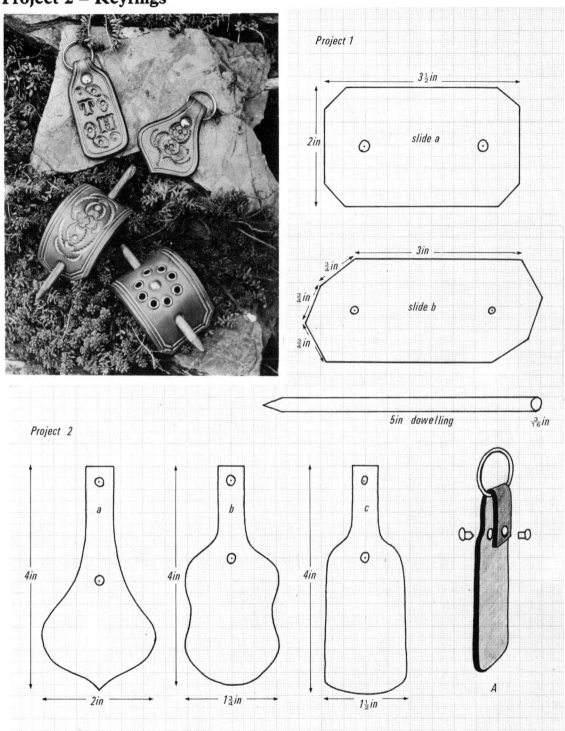

Project 1

slide a

3½in

2in

slide b

3in

¾in

¾in

¾in

5in dowelling

3/16 in

Project 2

a

b

c

4in

4in

4in

2in

1¾in

1½in

A

Project 3 – Crosses
and Pendants

You will need:

small pieces of scrap 3mm ($\frac{1}{8}$in) leather
small jeweller's ring
length of thong
knife
screw crease
number 3 edge shave
dye
piece of stiff card
six-way punch plier

Copy the design for the cross or pendant on to the card, and cut out. Using the card template, place it on the leather, and draw round. Cut out the leather, and punch a hole using the smallest gauge tube on the six-way punch plier. Set the screw crease and make a crease line if required. Bevel with the number 3 edge shave on both sides. Pattern if required, then dye and polish. Attach the thong by means of a small jeweller's ring placed through the hole at the top. Your pendant is then complete.

Project 4 – Wrist-band

You will need:

a piece of 3mm ($\frac{1}{8}$in) leather measuring roughly 7in (17·5cm) by 3in (75mm)
a small piece of $\frac{1}{8}$in (3mm) thong
knife
ruler
screw crease
number 3 edge shave
dye
piece of stiff card, roughly 7in (17·5cm) by 3in (75mm)
six-way punch plier

Copy your pattern on to the card, and cut out. Place the template on the leather, and draw round. Cut out the leather. Punch holes, using the number 4 tube on the six-way punch plier. Open the screw crease to approximately $\frac{1}{4}$in (6mm), and apply a crease line all the way round. Open the screw crease a further $\frac{1}{8}$in (3mm), and repeat. Now, with the number 3 edge shave, bevel all around on both front and back edges. Apply patterning by embossing or carving, and then dye and polish. Decorative stitching and studs should be applied after dyeing. When dyed and polished, burnish the edges, and insert the thong somewhat in the manner of a shoelace. Criss-cross, and your wrist-band is then complete.

Project 5 – Watch-strap

You will need:

one piece of 3mm ($\frac{1}{8}$in) leather measuring approximately 7in (17·5cm) by 2in (5cm)
one piece of 1$\frac{3}{4}$mm (about $\frac{1}{16}$in) leather, measuring approximately 10in (25cm) by 1in (25mm)
piece of card measuring 12in (30cm) by 8in (20cm)
six-way punch plier
knife
ruler
screw crease
number 3 edge shave
$\frac{5}{8}$in (15mm) slit punch
$\frac{5}{8}$in (15mm) brass buckle
rivet and cap

Copy patterns a and b on to the card, and cut out to make templates. Draw round template a on to the 3mm ($\frac{1}{8}$in) leather, and cut out. Do the same with template b on the 1$\frac{3}{4}$mm ($\frac{1}{16}$in) leather. Punch $\frac{5}{8}$in (15mm) slits into part a, and punch holes into part b, using the smallest tube on the six-way punch plier except for the hole marked 'x' – this should be punched with tube number five. Apply crease lines with the screw crease if required, and bevel edges on both sides with the number 3 edge shave, for both parts a and b. Apply any patterning required, unless using studs or stitching, then dye and polish. When dyed, burnish the edges of both parts, then attach the buckle to part b, with the tongue of the buckle passing through the large hole indicated by 'x'. Attach with the tubular rivet, and then thread part b through part a as illustrated in diagram A, and your watch-strap is complete.

Templates for Projects 3, 4 and 5 are on page 102.

Project 3 – Crosses and Pendants
Project 4 – Wrist-band
Project 5 – Watch-strap

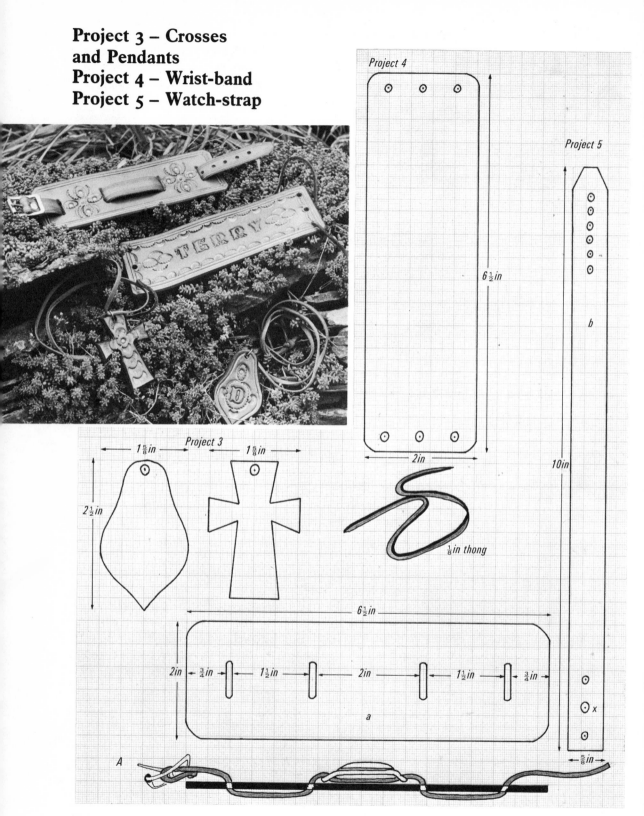

Project 4

6½in

2in

Project 5

b

10in

⅛in thong

Project 3

1⅝in   1⅝in

2½in

6½in

2in   ¾in   1½in   2in   1½in   ¾in

a

A

⅝in

x

Project 6 – Small Pleated Neck-purse

You will need:

a piece of 3mm ($\frac{1}{8}$in) leather measuring roughly 10in (25cm) by 5in (12·5cm)
4ft (1m) of 3mm ($\frac{1}{8}$in) thong
two eyelets
one press-stud
setting tool for press-stud
two number 2 egg-eyed harness needles
5-core linen thread
contact adhesive
dye
knife
screw crease
number 3 edge shave
ruler
stitch marker
awl
a piece of stiff card measuring roughly 10in (25cm) by 5in (12·5cm)

First, make the cardboard templates from the pattern, complete with holes, etc. Mark around templates on to the leather, and cut out parts a and b. Set the screw crease a $\frac{1}{4}$in (6mm) apart, and crease parts a and b all the way around. Now open the screw crease a further $\frac{1}{8}$in (3mm), and crease a second line across the top only of part b, and from the eyelet holes around the pointed flap on part a. Now, with the number 3 edge shave, bevel both sides of the parts that have a double crease line. Now punch holes. The two holes at the end of the cuts on part b should be made with the smallest tube of the six-way punch plier, and the two eyelet holes and the press-stud holes with the number 5 tube. Check this against your eyelets. Now that all the parts have been creased, edged, and have their holes punched, they may be dyed. Allow to dry, and apply varnish or polish. When this is done, attach eyelets to part a and press-stud base to part b, with the press-stud facing out through the grain side of the leather. Now parts a and b should be stitch-marked around the single crease lines, again on the grain side of the leather. Stitch-mark also $\frac{1}{8}$in (3mm) in from the cut lines on both sides. Now you are ready to start assembling the project. Turn side b flesh side up, and spread glue $\frac{1}{4}$in (6mm) wide on both sides of the cut lines. Allow to dry to the touch, then press the two edges of each cut line together to form a pleat, as shown in diagram A. Stitch together, using saddle stitch, until you have two pleats.

Now place side b to side a, flesh side to flesh side, and mark where the top of part b lies. Once this has been done, spread a line of glue ¼in (6mm) around the flesh side of parts a and b. Allow to dry to the touch, then stitch the two parts together with saddle stitch, forming a pouch as in the photograph. When the purse has been stitched together, trim off the excess leather, making both edges level. Then edge-level both back and front, and burnish all the edges. The thong can now be attached through the eyelets, and knotted on the inside. Finally, attach the press-stud with the top on the grain side of the flap, and the purse is complete.

Note: alternatively, this purse can be laced or thonged together – (see the sections on lacing and thonging in Chapter 4) – using Florentine, Whipstitch, Spanish Edge lace or Round Edge lacing.

Project 6 – Small
Pleated Neck-purse

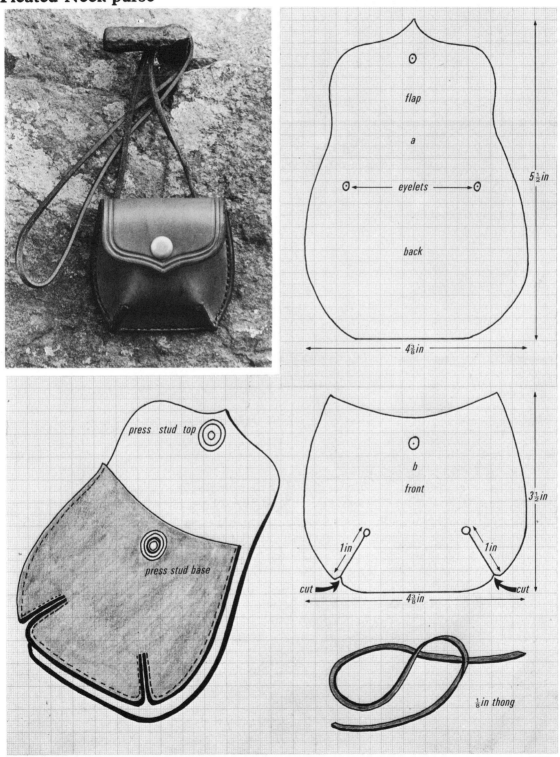

flap

a

○ ← eyelets → ○

back

$5\frac{1}{2}$ in

$4\frac{3}{8}$ in

press stud top

press stud base

b

front

$3\frac{1}{2}$ in

1 in

1 in

cut

cut

$4\frac{3}{8}$ in

$\frac{1}{8}$ in thong

Project 7 – Belt Pouch

You will need:

a piece of 3mm ($\frac{1}{8}$in) leather measuring 14in (35cm) by 6in (15cm)
a piece of 1$\frac{3}{4}$mm ($\frac{1}{16}$in) leather measuring 11in (27·5cm) by 2in (5cm)
press-stud and setting tool
four tubular rivets
5-core linen thread
beeswax
two number 2 egg-eyed harness needles
awl, dye, contact adhesive, stitch marker and screw crease
number 3 edge shave
knife and ruler
six-way punch plier
a piece of card measuring roughly 15in (37·5cm) by 8in (20cm)

Make cardboard templates from your pattern, and draw round parts a, b and d, copying part d twice, on the 3mm ($\frac{1}{8}$in) leather. Draw round part c on the 1$\frac{3}{4}$mm ($\frac{1}{16}$) leather. Cut out all five parts. Set the screw crease to $\frac{1}{4}$in (6mm), and crease round all parts. Open the screw crease a further $\frac{1}{8}$in (3mm), and double crease the top of part b front, on the vee line, and above the back line on the flap of part a. Also double crease both ends of gusset part c. Now edge-bevel all the double creased parts on both sides, and belt loops (parts d), on the grain side. Now all the holes should be punched, according to the size of your press-stud and tubular rivets. When this is done, all the parts can be dyed and varnished or polished. When dry, assembly can be started. First, stitch-mark along the single crease line on parts a and b. Then stud the two d parts into place on the back of part a, as indicated by the dotted line. The base of the press-stud should now be put into part b, facing out on the grain side. When this is done, spread a line of glue around the side and bottom on the flesh side of part b, and also along one side of the flesh side of the gusset part c. When the glue is dry to the touch, press the gusset c around the front of part b, forming half a purse. Saddle stitch into place, using about six stitches to the inch or 25mm. Once this is done, apply a line of glue to the other edge of the gusset on the flesh side, and also around the flesh side edge of the back of part a, below the back line corresponding with the stitch-marks. Then attach the back to the gusset, making sure it is symmetrical, and stitch into place. Attach the press-stud top to the flap, facing out on the flesh side, and trim off the leather around the stitched seams until a level edge is achieved. Then edge-shave both sides of the front and back edges, and finally burnish all the edges, thus completing the belt pouch.

Project 7 – Belt Pouch

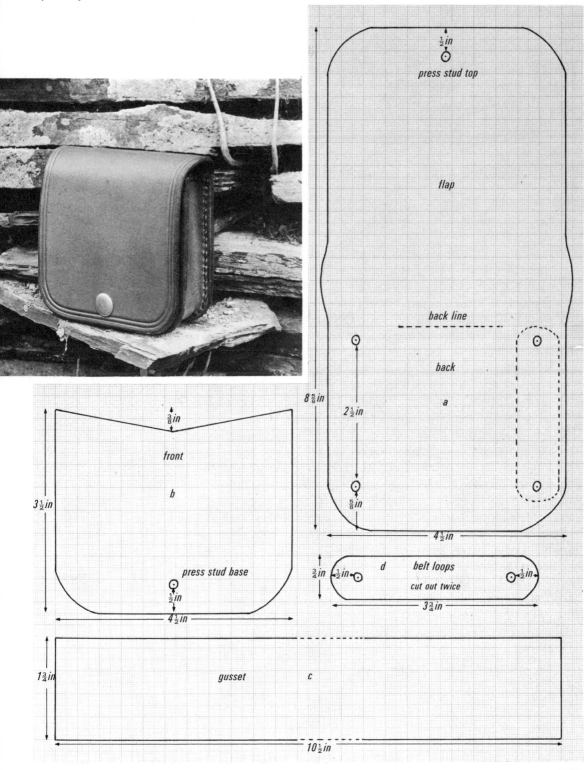

press stud top

flap

back line

back

a

$8\frac{5}{8}$ in

$2\frac{1}{2}$ in

$\frac{1}{2}$ in

$\frac{5}{8}$ in

$4\frac{1}{2}$ in

front

$\frac{3}{8}$ in

b

$3\frac{1}{2}$ in

press stud base

$\frac{1}{2}$ in

$4\frac{1}{2}$ in

$\frac{3}{4}$ in $\frac{1}{2}$ in   d   belt loops

cut out twice

$\frac{1}{2}$ in

$3\frac{3}{4}$ in

gusset   c

$1\frac{3}{4}$ in

$10\frac{1}{2}$ in

Project 8 – Three-plait
Trick Weave Belt

You will need:

a strip of 3mm ($\frac{1}{8}$in) leather $1\frac{1}{2}$in ($3 \cdot 7$cm) wide by 55in ($1 \cdot 4$m) long
a $1\frac{1}{2}$in ($3 \cdot 7$cm) belt buckle
four tub rivets
dye
piece of stiff card
knife and ruler
six-way punch plier
screw crease
number 3 edge shave
a 1in ($2 \cdot 5$cm) slit punch

First, make a template out of card from the pattern. Then cut your strip of leather $1\frac{1}{2}$in ($3 \cdot 7$cm) wide, using either a plough gauge or a knife and ruler. Determine the length of belt you require, bearing in mind that when it is plaited it will reduce by about a fifth, so make sure the extra amount is added to the length. Now trace around template a, the buckle end, on to the leather strip, and then trace template b, the tongue end, on to the other end of the leather strip. Now cut the ends out, and then the plaiting, using a knife and ruler. This should leave you with three $\frac{1}{2}$in (12mm) strips down the centre of the belt length. Using the number 3 tube punch on your punch plier, punch two cut holes at each end of the cut lines, plus six rivet holes at the buckle end. Now cut the slit for the buckle tongue, and punch the holes at the tongue end of the belt length. The size of the holes should be determined by the buckle used. Set the screw crease at about $\frac{1}{4}$in (6mm), and make a crease line on each end of the belt from where the lines have been cut for the plaiting, and on the keeper (c). Open the screw crease a further $\frac{1}{8}$in (3mm), and make a second crease line. Now, with the number 3 edge shave, bevel all the belt edges on both sides, and the sides of the three plaiting strips. When this is done, punch the two holes in the keeper, using tube number 3, and then dye all the pieces. When you have finished dyeing and polishing, plait up the thonging as shown in the decorative section on *Weaving and Plaiting* in Chapter 5. Wrap the keeper around and stud together with the tubular rivet, then attach the buckle. Burnish the edges of the belt to complete.

Project 8 – Three-plait Trick Weave Belt

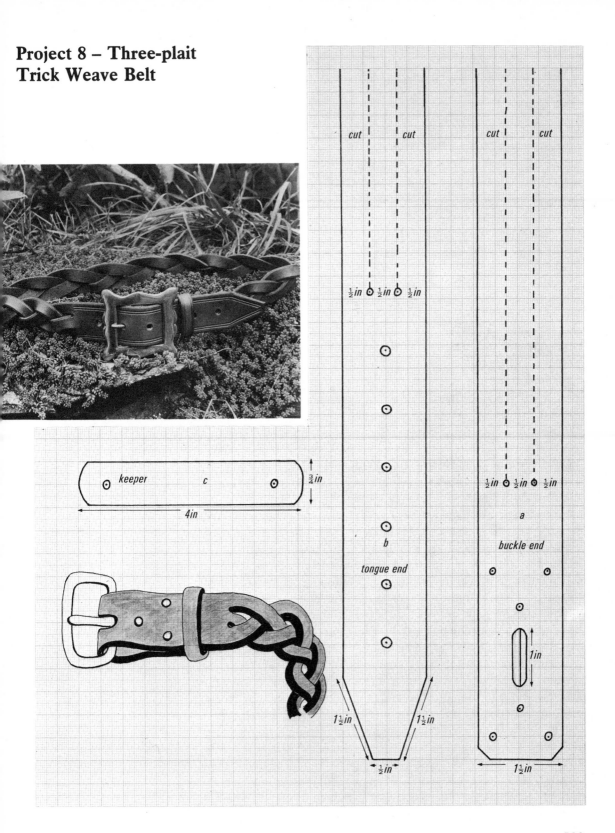

cut | cut | cut | cut

½in ⊙ ½in ⊙ ½in

½in ⊙ ½in ⊙ ½in

keeper | c | ¾in

4in

a

buckle end

b

tongue end

1in

1½in | 1½in

½in

1½in

Project 9 –
Front-fastening Belt

You will need:

a strip of 3mm ($\frac{1}{8}$in) leather measuring $1\frac{3}{4}$in (4·3cm) by 55in (1·4m)

a strip of 4mm ($\frac{1}{8}$in) leather measuring 24in (60cm) by 2in (5cm)

a strip of $1\frac{3}{4}$mm ($\frac{1}{16}$in) leather measuring $\frac{1}{2}$in (12mm) by 10in (25cm)

a 1in (2·5cm) belt buckle.

seven tubular rivets and caps

5-core linen thread

beeswax

two number 2 egg-eyed harness needles

stitch marker

awl

six-way punch plier

screw crease

number 3 edge shave

knife and ruler

a 1in (2·5cm) slit punch

contact adhesive

stiff card

First determine the length of the belt on part a. The leather should overlap itself by about 5in (12·5cm). Now copy all the parts on to the card, and make templates of parts a, b, c, d, e and f. Trace round all these on to the leather – part a on to each end of the 55in (1·4m) strip, parts b and c onto the 24in (60cm) strip, and parts d, e and f on to the 10in (25cm) strip. Remember to mark all the holes, slits, etc. When all the pieces have been cut out, set the screw crease to the desired width and put double crease lines on all the parts. Then with the number 3 edge shave, bevel both sides of all the edges, except the flesh side of parts c and b where they are to be sewn. Punch all the holes and slits, using tube 3 or 4, and then dye all the parts. Polish or varnish, and when dry you will be ready to assemble. First stitch-mark parts c and b, where they are to be sewn, using about six stitches to the inch or 25mm. Now wrap keepers around, and stud the ends together with tubular rivets. Slide keepers d and e on to part c, and then slide keeper f on to part c. Attach the buckle with two tubular rivets, so that the buckle as well as keeper f are sandwiched in the bend of part c, in front of the rivets. Now, using the templates of parts b and c, mark their position on part a (the main body of the belt) including holes 1a and 1b from template c. When this has been done, make a few scratches with the point of your knife on part a, where parts b and

Project 9 –
Front-fastening Belt

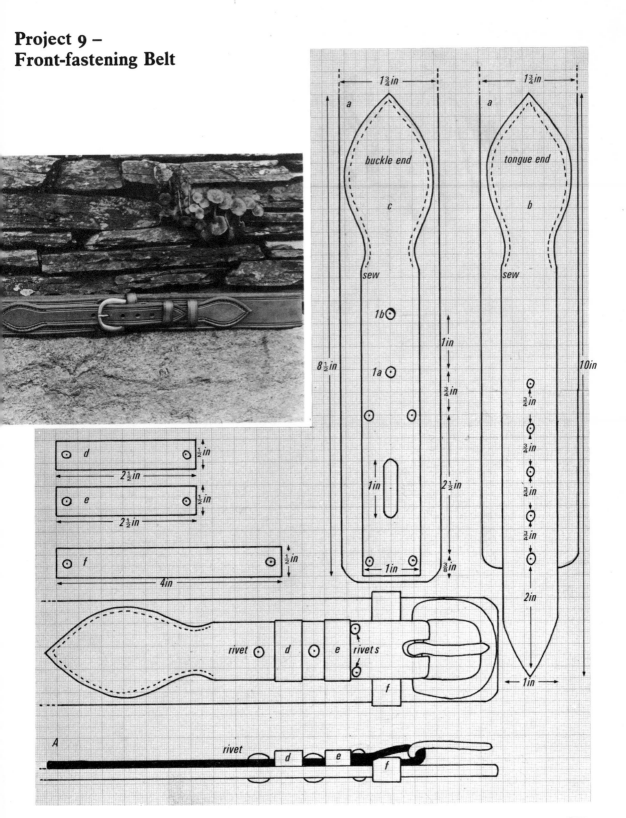

c are to be stitched. Now apply glue to the grain side of part a, on the scratched area, and also to the flesh sides of parts b and c. When dry to the touch, push into place and stitch, using a saddle stitch. When both parts are stitched into place, take part a at the buckle end and push in through keeper f, so that keeper f appears on the flesh side of part f, as shown in the cross-section in diagram A. Slide keepers d and e into place and attach tubular rivets, so that they go through both pieces of leather a and c, as shown in diagram A. Finally, burnish all the edges of the belt to complete.

Project 10 – Daisy Bag

You will need:

approximately 3 sq. ft. (28 sq. cm) of 3mm ($\frac{1}{8}$in) leather
a 1in (25mm) buckle
two 1in (25mm) dee rings
a 1in (25mm) leather strap (of own design)
a small scrap of $1\frac{3}{4}$mm ($\frac{1}{16}$in) leather measuring $2\frac{1}{2}$in (5cm) by $\frac{1}{2}$in (12mm)
5-core thread
contact adhesive
two number 2 egg-eyed harness needles
stitch-marker
screw crease
number 3 edge shave
a $\frac{3}{4}$in (18mm) slit punch
six-way punch plier
sheet of stiff card
dye and varnish
knife and ruler
beeswax
skiving knife

Make all the template parts from the card, using this pattern. Make sure all the parts are marked for dee rings, buckles, and so on. Place the templates on to the leather, and trace round. You will need to trace two of part b (side). Then cut out all the parts. Part d (keeper) should be cut from the $1\frac{3}{4}$mm ($\frac{1}{16}$in) leather – all the others from the 3mm ($\frac{1}{8}$in). Set the screw crease to $\frac{1}{4}$in (6mm), and crease a further $\frac{1}{8}$in (3mm), and make a second crease line from the stitch line (17in (42·5cm) up) on part a, around the flap and on the curve above the buckle; on part b, on the top where the leather goes in; on the tongue part c, up to the curve where it is to be stitched; and on keeper d. Punch slit in part e, and then edge bevel with the number 3 edge shave all the parts having a double crease line, on both sides. When this has been done, all the parts can be dyed and varnished. When they are dry you can start stitch-marking; first stitch-mark part a, up to the stitch line on both sides. Stitch-mark the top curved part of the tongue (part c), half of the buckle holder (part e) and half of the dee ring holder (part f). The stitching is marked on the pattern, at a spacing of six stitches to the inch or 25mm. When you have marked all the parts, place the template of part f on to part b, where shown by a broken line. Do the same with parts e and c, on part a. Mark round them all, then with the point of the knife score inside the marked areas lightly, to make a good surface for bonding with the adhesive.

Next take the skiving knife and skive off the half which has not been stitch-marked of both dee ring holders, plus the half of the buckle holder (part e) which has not been stitch marked. Apply adhesive to the flesh side of the dee ring holders, and when touch-dry, slip the dee rings over into the centres of the curves, with the straight sides of the dee rings on the flesh sides, and push together. Then glue in place on the two sides (b) and stitch in place. Next, wrap round keeper, and stud together. Apply adhesive to the flesh side of the buckle holder (part e), and when dry to the touch put the buckle in the centre and slip on the keeper, so that it comes over the stitch-marked side. Push the buckle holder together, and glue and stitch in place on part c. Now apply adhesive to the flesh side of part c (tongue) adjacent to the stitch-marked part, and glue and stitch in place on part a. You should now have three parts – two part b's (sides) and one part a (front and flap). Apply adhesive in a line about $\frac{1}{8}$in (6mm) on the flesh side of part a, adjacent to where it is stitch-marked, and on the flesh side of one of the part b's – on both sides and the bottom, but not the top where the double crease line is. Allow adhesive to dry to the touch; then, starting from the bottom buckle end of part a, press to part b where marked. Press together all the way round, and then stitch in place. This should give you a half a box shape; repeat in the same way for the other side, and you should have the complete bag. Trim off any overhanging leather on the seams, to give a level edge, and then edge-shave all the seamed edges on both sides. Dye these in and burnish, and finally attach the strap to the dee rings by means of press-studs, tubular rivets, or stitching, to complete the bag.

Note: the assembly method for this bag is shown in the photostrip, 'making a single-compartment bag' at the end of Chapter 4. Study this before commencing the project.

Project 10 – Daisy Bag

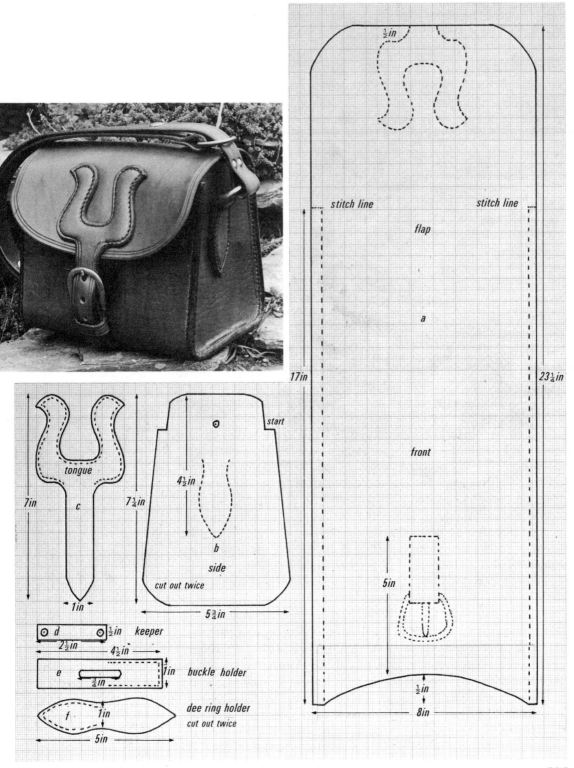

½in

stitch line   stitch line

flap

a

17in   23¼in

start

front

4½in

tongue

7in   c   7½in

b

side

cut out twice

1in   5¾in

5in

d   ½in   keeper

2½in

4½in

e   1in   buckle holder
        ¾in

dee ring holder
cut out twice

f   1in

½in

5in   8in

Project 11 –
Square Bag
with Front Pocket

You will need:

a piece of 3mm ($\frac{1}{8}$in) leather measuring approximately 48in (120cm) by 12in (30cm)
a piece of $\frac{3}{4}$mm ($\frac{1}{16}$in) leather measuring approximately 36in (90cm) by 5in (12·5cm)
two 1in (25mm) dee rings
6-core linen thread
two number 2 egg-eyed harness needles
awl
stitch-marker
knife and ruler
screw crease
number 3 edge shave
dye and varnish
large piece of stiff card
a race (or tool for making a groove)
four tubular rivets
two press-studs

Cut the templates for all the parts from the pattern, then trace around the templates on to the leather – parts a, b, c, d, e, f, g, h, j and k on to the 3mm ($\frac{1}{8}$in), and parts l and m on to the $1\frac{3}{4}$mm ($\frac{1}{16}$in). When all the parts have been cut out, set the screw crease to $\frac{1}{4}$in (6mm) and screw crease round all the parts. Open the screw crease a further $\frac{1}{8}$in (3mm) and crease with a second line part a, from the front line around the flap; part b, across the top vee cut; part c, all round; part d, across the vee cut top; part e, all round; part f, all round; parts g and h, all round; part j, along the middle leaving 1in (25mm) at each end; also crease just the tags where they are cut in on part m, and the two ends on part l. With the number 3 edge shave, bevel all the edges with a double crease line, on both sides. Now all the parts are ready to be dyed. When dyed and varnished, you are ready to start assembling them. First stitch-mark, at six stitches to the inch or 25mm, around part a on the back below the front line, where it has been crease-lined only once. Stitch-mark part b on each side above $4\frac{1}{2}$in (112mm), where the broken line is shown on the pattern. To stitch-mark part c you will need to measure $\frac{1}{2}$in (12mm) in from the straight edge, where it is cut in. This should be stitch-marked on the flesh side. On part d, stitch-mark the sides and bottom, where there is a single crease line. For part e, measure $2\frac{1}{2}$in (62mm) down from the square end, and stitch-mark the two sides and the end. On part j, stitch-mark the two ends where there is a single line. Finally, stitch-mark half of part k, and on one side of part l. Having done all that, begin attaching the parts by glueing and stitching part e on to part a where indicated by the broken line on the pattern. Remember when sticking the parts together to score lightly the surfaces to be joined, to give a better adhesion. Stick both the dee rings into their holders (k) and then stitch to part m where indicated. Glue and stitch part j to part d where indicated; this should appear bent in the middle. When this has been done, stitch part l (pocket gusset) – the side which has not been stitch-marked – around part d (pocket front), making a half purse. Now take part f and glue the flesh side ½in (12mm) down from the square end, and stick it in the centre of the pocket flap on the grain side of the leather. Parts f and c should appear grain side up. Now glue along the groin side, ½in (12mm) from the edge, along part c, where indicated by the broken line, and part b where indicated. When the glue is dry to the touch, push these two parts together. The pocket flap (c) should face up over the top of part b (inside front), and part f should be sandwiched in between parts c and b. Now stitch along the stitch-marked line, which should be facing upwards on the flesh side. When this is done you should end up with parts a, b, d and m, plus the straps. Parts g, h, and all the other parts should be stitched on to parts a, b, d and m. Now glue part d on to part b by the gusset, around below the pocket flap stitch-mark line. The stitch-marks on the gusset (l) should go round the sides and bottom of part b (inside front). Now take part m (the bag gusset) and spread ¼in (6mm) of glue along the flesh side on one edge; also on part b, glue ¼in (6mm) around the flesh sides and bottom. Then push the gusset (m) on to the front (b), and stitch round the complete front using the stitch-marks at the top of part b, above where the pocket flap is stitched on, and running on to the stitch-marks on part l (pocket gusset). When both sides and the bottom are stitched in place, the back part a should be glued and stitched on to the other edge of the bag gusset (part m). Check diagram A to see where all the parts go. All the seamed edges should now be trimmed and chamfered with a piece of medium sandpaper, until the leather edges are all level. Then with the number 3 edge shave, bevel all these edges on each side. Dye in and burnish. Finally, attach the two press-studs, tops to part h where indicated, bottoms to part g where indicated, and attach to the bag by other ends with tubular rivets to complete. If you want the strap to be adjustable, vary the spacing of the press-studs accordingly.

Project 11 –
Square Bag
with Front Pocket

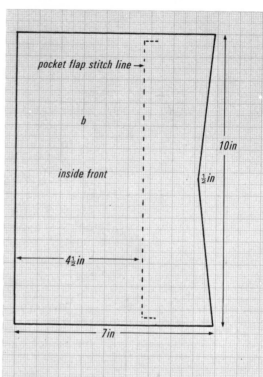

pocket flap stitch line →

b

inside front

10in

$\frac{1}{2}$in

$4\frac{1}{2}$in

7in

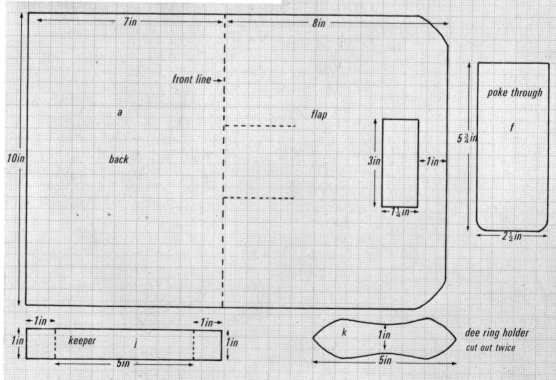

7in

8in

front line →

a

flap

back

10in

3in

1in

$1\frac{1}{4}$in

poke through

f

$5\frac{3}{4}$in

$2\frac{1}{2}$in

← 1in →

← 1in →

1in

keeper   j

1in

5in

k   1in

5in

dee ring holder
cut out twice

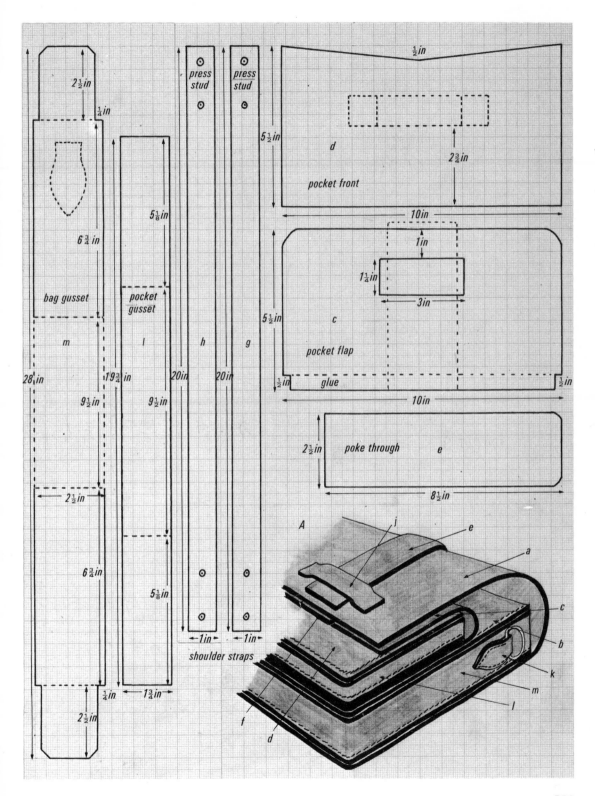

$2\frac{1}{2}in$

$\frac{1}{4}in$

$6\frac{3}{4}in$

bag gusset

m

$28in$

$9\frac{1}{2}in$

$2\frac{1}{2}in$

$6\frac{3}{4}in$

$\frac{1}{4}in$

$2\frac{1}{2}in$

$5\frac{1}{8}in$

pocket gusset

l

$19\frac{3}{4}in$

$9\frac{1}{2}in$

$5\frac{1}{8}in$

$1\frac{3}{4}in$

press stud

h

$20in$

press stud

g

$20in$

$1in$

$1in$

shoulder straps

$\frac{1}{2}in$

pocket front

d

$5\frac{1}{2}in$

$2\frac{3}{4}in$

$10in$

$1in$

$1\frac{1}{4}in$

$3in$

pocket flap

c

$5\frac{1}{2}in$

$\frac{1}{2}in$ glue $\frac{1}{2}in$

$10in$

poke through e

$2\frac{1}{2}in$

$8\frac{1}{2}in$

A

i

e

a

c

b

k

m

l

f

d

119

Safety

Here I should like to impress upon you the importance of safety, for many of the tools, dyes, finishes and cleaners used in leather-work are potentially dangerous.

First, *Tools*. Leather knives should be very sharp to give you the best edge on your cut leather, so these should obviously be kept well out of the reach of children. Great care should also be taken when using them; you should always cut on board, never in your lap, or in the air.

Second, *Dyes*. These should also be kept well out of the reach of children. The spirit variety are highly poisonous, as well as being extremely inflammable. Never keep dyes in lemonade bottles without first removing the labels, and marking them as being both poisonous and inflammable, as they could easily be mistaken for whatever was previously in the bottle. Dyes should also be used in a well-ventilated area, as the fumes given off can often be danger-ous. At NO time should you smoke, or use dyes near a naked flame or any intense heat.

Glues are also highly inflammable, and the fumes given off by neoprene-based glues can damage your eyes and lungs. So please take care to follow the manufacturer's instructions, to be found on the tin or jar. Always replace the tops on glues, dyes and finishes, as this not only saves them from evaporating, but also prevents them being spilt, or even drunk by children or pets.

Cleaners, such as the one which I have discussed making from oxalic acid crystals, are extremely poisonous, and great care should be taken when making up this liquid. Never leave the crystals lying around where they could be picked up and eaten. Always wash your hands after using the cleaner, and keep applicators in a jar on a high shelf.

The key to safety is common sense. Dangerous tools and liquids should be kept on a high shelf in your workshop. Knives should be kept in a box or drawer, and it is a simple task to make a sheath for knives out of scrap leather. It is also good practice. Always keep a small but comprehensive first aid box in your workshop, or at hand where you work. The best way to enjoy leatherwork is safely, both for yourself and others.

Afterword

In this book I have tried to awaken in you, the reader, a desire to create your own leatherwork, and to develop your own skills. While I have been working towards completing this 'opus', it has at times been frustrating, as it is not easy to convey something which you can do with your hands on to paper for another person to follow. My original concept was to write the book as if I had invited each one of you into my workshop, and was instructing you personally. I hope that this has succeeded.

I have gained immense satisfaction from the work I have done for the book, and hope that when you come to make your first projects you in turn will gain the same kind of satisfaction, as all leatherworkers do, from having made something from scratch with your own hands. Leatherwork is very rewarding; it is a skill which you never stop developing, whether making things for yourself, or items to be sold professionally.

I have tried to impress upon you that you should let your own imagination and personality show in your work, for this is the only way in which to express truly the craft of leatherworking. At times you will come up against problems, but these are never insurmountable. There are books, and other craftsmen about, who will always help you to overcome such difficulties. The idea of leatherwork is to enhance the hide – always bear this in mind. Never cover up the fact that it is leather.

Always try to seek out other craftsmen, and talk to them, look at their work; it will often inspire you to produce better work. A real craftsman will never be afraid to show you how to do things, for we all have the same thing in common, a love of leather, and so shall enjoy and explore its possibilities together.

I.H-H.

Bibliography

The following are books on leather and leatherwork which may be of further interest to the reader:

Leather Secrets F.O. Baird
The Leathercraftsman Inc., P.O. Box 1386, Fort Worth, Texas 76101, U.S.A. First printed 1951, revised edition 1976

General Leatherwork Raymond Cherry
McKnight & McKnight Publishing Company, Bloomington, Illinois, U.S.A. First published 1940

Leather John W. Waterer
Clarendon Press, Oxford. Reprinted from Singer & Holmyard: History & Technology

Saddlery and Harness Making Edited by Paul N. Hasluck
J. A. Allen & Co. Ltd., 1 Lower Grosvenor Place, London S.W.1. 1962. From the original edition 1904, Cassell & Co. Ltd.

Leatherwork F. R. Smith, F.R.S.A.,
Pitman & Sons Ltd., London. First published 1930, reprinted 1945

Leather Braiding Bruce Grant
Cornell Maritime Press Inc., Cambridge, Maryland, U.S.A. 1961

Encyclopedia of Rawhide Work and Leather Braiding Bruce Grant
Cornell Maritime Press Inc., Cambridge, Maryland, U.S.A. 1971

Modern Leather Design Donald J. Wilcox
Watson Guptill, New York, U.S.A. 1969

Contemporary Leather Donna Z. Meilach
Henry Regnery Company, Chicago, Illinois, U.S.A. 1971

How to Colour Leather Al Stohlman
The Leathercraftsman Inc., P.O. Box 1386, Fort Worth, Texas 76101, U.S.A. 1961

Tech Tips Al Stohlman
Craftool Co., Fort Worth, Texas 76101, U.S.A. 1969

Leathercraft Eileen C. Greenwood
E. & F. N. Spon Ltd., London 1949

Black Jack and Leather Bottles O. Baker
Privately printed, Cheltenham. 1921

Leather: in Life, Art and Industry J. W. Waterer
Faber & Faber, London. 1946

Leather D. J. Wilcox and J. S. Manning
Pitman Ltd., London. 1974

Leather Tooling and Carving Chris H. Groneman
Dover Publications Inc., New York, U.S.A. 1974

The Leathercraft Book Pat Hills and Joan Wiener
Robert Hale Ltd., London. 1973

Leathercraft W. A. Attwater
B. T. Batsford Ltd., London. 1961

Leather Art F. O. Baird
American Handicrafts Co., U.S.A. 1946

List of Suppliers

A catalogue is available on request from those suppliers marked with an asterisk.

Europe

British Isles

Channel Islands
*Gruts — All leathercraft supplies
35 The Pollet
St Peters Port
Guernsey

England
*The Joseph Dixon Tool Co. Ltd. — Saddlery tools
Bott Lane, Walsall, Staffs.

*S. Glassner — Tools and fittings
68 Worple Road,
Wimbledon, London SW19 4HX

*Taylor & Co. Tools Ltd. — Tools, machinery and fittings
54 Old Street,
London E.C.1.

*Craftwares Ltd. — All leather supply and tools, Tandy franchise for U.K., and fittings
Nassau Mills, Patricroft,
Manchester M30 0QJ

*D. A. Friend — Full leather supplies, tools and fittings
Brighton, England

*J. Crogan & Sons — Fittings, buckles, tools; one of the two oak bark tanneries in Europe
Manor Tannery,
Grampound Road, St. Austell,
Cornwall

Bakers Tannery — Oak bark tanners
Colliton,
Devon

Wiggins Thomas (Beefeater) Ltd. — Vegetable tanned leather (good for carving)
Ratcliffe Cross Street,
Tower Hamlets, London E.1.

Connolly Bros. (Curriers) Ltd. — Tannery for all types of leather and suede
39 Chalton Street,
London N.W.1.

*Parker Toggles 23 Fournier Street, London E.1.	Fittings, press-studs, thread
Rose Fittings City Road, London E.C.1.	Fittings and sundries
Gedge & Co. (Clerkenwell) Ltd. 88 St. John Street, London E.C.1.	Dyes and dye powders, varnish
Pronk, Davis & Rusby Ltd. 44 Penton Street, London N.1.	Dyes, water and spirit; powder samples available
Leveritt and Pearce Ltd. 96 Webber Street, London S.E.1.	Dyes, polishes and finishes
John Myland Ltd. 80 Norwood High Street, London SE27 GNW	Dyes and varnishes
*Stanley Bros. In Town Row, Walsall, Staffs.	Buckle manufacturers; will cast to your own design
*Samuel Price Ltd. Tantara Street Works, Tantara Street, Walsall, Staffs.	Buckle manufacturers
Matthew Harvey Ltd. Bath Street Works, Bath Street, Walsall, Staffs.	Brass founders

Scotland

*Andrew Patterson & Co. Ltd. 12–15 St. Andrews Square, Glasgow.	Tools, leather fittings
National Chrome Tanning Co. (1936) Ltd. Locher Works, Bridge-on-Weir.	Chrome tanned leathers

Denmark

*Laeder Og Skind Specialforretningen Vankunsten 3, København.	Leather, fittings, supplies

128

France
*Blanchard Tool Co. Paris.	Tools; very good quality

Germany
*Kromwell Pelart C-MBH 8500, Neurenburg.	All leathercraft supplies
*Fachverband Kurzwaren Kornerstrasse 41, 58 Hagen, (Westf).	Leather, fittings, buckles

United States of America

*Tandy Leather Co. 8117 Highway 80 West, Fort Worth, Texas 76116	The most comprehensive range of leathercraft supplies; 100-page catalogue – to see it is to believe it!
*Sax Crafts 1103 North 3rd Street, Milwaukee, Wisconsin	Tools and supplies
A. C. Products Co. Ltd. 422 Hudson Street, New York City, New York 10014	Leather suppliers
*Fiebing Chemical Company 516 South Second Street, Milwaukee, Wisconsin	Dyes and finishes
*Colo Craft Leathercraft 1310 South Broadway, Denver, Colorado 80210	Leather, tools, fittings
*North & Judd Manufacturing Co. New Britain, Connecticut	Buckles and fittings
*Henry Westfal Co. 4, East 32nd Street, New York City, New York 10016	Tools and supplies; distributor for C.S. Osbourne tools
*MacPherson Brothers 730 Polk Street, San Francisco, California 94100	Tools and leather

The Tannery	Leather and tools
49 Grove Street,	
New York City,	
New York 10001	
Mac Leather	Leather suppliers
424 Broom Street	
New York City	
New York 10013	

Australasia

Australia

The following are craft associations and wholesalers:—

The Craft Association of Victoria
350 Victoria Street,
North Melbourne,
Victoria 3051

The Craft Centre
309 Toorak Road,
South Yarra,
Victoria 3141

Craft Association of Queensland
37 Leichhardt Street,
Brisbane,
Queensland 4000

Craft Association of Western Australia
34 Cliff Street,
Fremantle,
Western Australia 6160

Craft Association of New South Wales
26 King Street,
Sydney,
New South Wales 2000

Craft Centre
33 Brighton Avenue,
Croydon Park,
New South Wales 2133

The Craft Warehouse
Martin Avenue,
Sydney,
New South Wales 2000

Craft Association of Tasmania
Salamanca Place,
Hobart,
Tasmania 7000

Craft Association of South Australia
167 Payneham Road,
St. Peters,
South Australia 5069

The Craft Centre
26 Gilbert Place,
Adelaide,
South Australia 5000

New Zealand
The following are tool and material suppliers:—

Goulding Industries Handcraft Centre
158 Cuba St.,
PO Box 9022,
Wellington

Best Leatherware Ltd.
400 Queen St.,
Auckland 1

Creative Craft Supplies
14 Milford Rd.,
Milford,
Auckland 9

Little Crow Ltd.
Handcraft Supplies,
272 Parnell Rd.,
Parnell,
Auckland 1

Handcraft Supplies
Arcade 70,
Hurstmere Road,
Takapuna

Te Matenga – Leathercraft
585 Fergusson Drive,
Upper Hutt

Hookers Handcraft Supplies 1974 Ltd.
123 Victoria St.,
Hamilton

The Tasman Tanning Co Ltd.
424 St. Asaph St.,
Christchurch

Handcraft Supplies NZ Ltd.
13–15 Rosebank Rd.,
Avondale,
Auckland

Index

Design Notes

Design Notes